What is the future for mankind, doom and destruction or hope and harmony? *After Nostradamus* traces the course of prophecy down the ages and examines this question in the light of the words of the great visionaries and prophets of the past.

After Nostradamus

A. Woldben

Translated from the Italian
by Gavin Gibbons

Mayflower

Granada Publishing Limited
Published in 1975 by Mayflower Books Ltd
Frogmore, St Albans, Herts AL2 2NF

First published in Great Britain by
Neville Spearman Ltd 1973
Copyright © Neville Spearman 1973
Copyright © Edizioni Mediterranee 1972
Made and printed in Great Britain by
Richard Clay (The Chaucer Press) Ltd
Bungay, Suffolk
Set in Linotype Pilgrim

Contents

TRANSLATOR'S FOREWORD

This is a fascinating book, as it traces the story of prophecy down the ages, the greatest amount of space being given, not unexpectedly to the best-known prophet of all, Michele Nostradamus. It is important to realize that all prophets have certain limitations. There are ideas which their listeners cannot understand and which have to be modified and described in the terms of their day; an obvious example is an air raid, which in medieval or early modern terms becomes fire or darts from the sky. But there are also concepts which are beyond the ability of the prophet himself to visualize. What man in the sixteenth century could understand the idea of a republic? – even though the idea had been suggested in classical days. The so-called Roman Republic did not, indeed, have a king, but it was an oligarchy and quite unlike the modern republics which first appeared at the end of the eighteenth century. An even more recent example is the drawing together of the nations of which the European Common Market is the best known and most exciting – an idea which was just an idyllic dream even in the early twentieth century. When we read the Bible we realize how Jesus taught ideas which are true for all time – but he always clothed them in first-century terms.

Readers in non-Catholic countries will probably not understand why there is so much reference to the Papacy. They will not realize, perhaps, what an important temporal power was enjoyed by the Popes right up to the unification of Italy in 1861. But the Roman Catholic church today still enjoys a place in countries where it is the religion of the majority of the people, which is difficult for those in other countries to understand. It forms a stabilizing and moderating influence and unfortunately, all too often, has been stubbornly opposed to reform until quite recent years.

There is a much deeper meaning to this book. God has not declared that the fearful things forecast for the last quarter of the twentieth century are certainties. Time and time again we are told that man will bring them on himself. One only has to think of the low standards of the present age, and the decline in the respect for moral standards. Basic human kindness is much less, and despite all the protection by the state, the big still prey on the small, both as giant industrial and business concerns, and as the state itself, which has become too powerful and pries into every detail of the life of the average man. Law is not respected as more and more it tends to protect the new monsters from the ordinary man and less and less the innocent man from the criminal – indeed so often when a man in despair turns to the Church, he finds it obsessed with happenings in distant Africa and less concerned with the events going on round about it. Indeed, the more permissive churchmen condone crime and deplore punishment as bad for the criminal!

But even today there is hope. The fearful dangers of a Third World War do seem to have frightened the nations of the world into drawing together. There are friendly approaches between the giant powers, and American statesmen visit Russia and China, which would have been unheard of even in the mid-twentieth century. While this translation was being made, official peace came to one of the world's trouble spots, Vietnam, and it will only be a matter of time before the actual fighting will cease altogether. Everyone wants peace and the most promising movement for the future has begun in Europe itself, scene of so much bloody fighting in the first half of the twentieth century, where the European Common Market was set up in 1958 and which has now expanded from six to nine members. War between the Western European countries is now unthinkable. The success of this community will be a shining example to other nations of the world to unite and eventually all these groupings will fuse together as one United Planet Earth.

But we are not out of the wood yet. This is where a book like the present one is so valuable. We have been told down the centuries what will happen if Man does not learn to control his lower instincts. After the end of the Wars of the Roses at the Battle of Bosworth in 1485, internal peace and unity seemed to have come to England and Wales, especially after the political union of the two in 1536. But the Civil War broke out again in 1642 and a bitter campaign was fought all over Great Britain, for which defences, which had crumbled away with the neglect of 150 years, had to be hastily rebuilt. Indeed it was not until the Battle of Clifton by Penrith in 1745 and the massacre of Culloden Moor the following year that land fighting came to an end in Great Britain – two and a half centuries after the end of the Wars of the Roses. In 1940 land invasion was expected once more and there were air raids and coastal bombardments in both World Wars. Even today urban guerrilla warfare still threatens the ordinary man – such as is going on in Ireland.

. We have been fully warned by the prophecies. If we are to avoid the fearful happenings which have been foretold we must make a change in ourselves. We are so cynical and disillusioned today that we have lost the power to rejoice. So many of us have lost the ability even to be happy! We need look no further back than 1 January 1973, when Great Britain entered the European Common Market, to see how deep this determined pessimism and disillusion has got hold of the average man. The end of the World Wars in 1918 and 1945 were marked with national rejoicing, but the day when Great Britain banned for ever wars with her eight fellow-members of the Community, and the probable permanent end of fighting came for Western Europe, went off with only a few lame official celebrations. The man in the street said 'sell-out', 'watch the Russians' or shrugged his shoulders in complete indifference.

This bored, cynical indifference is the biggest danger to the future happiness of mankind. We must once again find a sense of wonder. Cynicism, superciliousness and boredom do not bring happiness but make life just that little more horrible. For the secret to the Happy Life lies in *ourselves*. An exciting attitude to life, known as Positive Thought, has sprung up in various parts of the world as an answer to the dreary grey cynicism and pessimism. In the United States it is known as Positive Thinking and is preached by Dr. Norman Vincent Peale in the Marble Church in New York. His books have sold millions of copies all over the world. Two people can be in the same situation. One will concentrate on all the bad aspects, the other on all the good ones. The latter will soon solve his problems – for he will soon find that many of them, approached in a Positive way, are no longer problems.

The greatest inspiration of all is God Himself. This is where every reader can help. By realizing the wonder of the Universe and of Divine Power, he will help to bring about a little more happiness and goodwill in a world where it is badly needed. He will help to avoid the terrors prophesied for so long but will still be able to bring us into that close relationship with God and to rise on to the Higher Plane where eventually we shall become – as so vividly described by Signor Voldben in Chapter 15 of this book – so full of love and understanding that we shall be in complete unity with God and enjoy with Him the Great Life for ever.

Gavin Gibbons
Shrewsbury.
26 February 1973

INTRODUCTION

*If laws are given, and judge-
ments carried out, the rest
will follow.* St. Augustine.

In these pages the principal prophecies have been collected, which refer to times yet to come. They are
culled from a number of sources and on the whole
reveal a striking similarity about the chief events which
will take place at the end of the century.

In describing these events we have intentionally
ignored the chronological order. No one knows what
it is, least of all those who have tried to construct a
calendar of fantasy by putting a date to these events.

The chaos of the present times does not encourage
us to expect any good in the immediate future. Most
of the prophecies foretell increasing disorder and confusion. Indeed they forecast the continual but necessary
break-up of life itself, just as the grain of seed has
first to fester in the ground in order to become the ear
and then bread. In the human sphere everything must
be changed completely to achieve life: otherwise it
will not be life but death. But the person who renews
himself will know how to live, as he will have himself
passed all the phases of decay.

According to all the prophecies, during the next
thirty years the world will pass through terrible tribulations. The necessity of renewal will first lead to the
destruction of everything we know in our present
civilization, to give way, in a second phase, to the
building of a fundamentally different society.

Those who have eyes to see and minds to understand
with will realize that what has been forecast is already
coming to pass. For years we have helped to take down

the old building stone by stone, and watched the collapse of the columns which held it up securely. The family, the state, authority, religion and society have sunk to a position which only a short time ago, would have been impossible to imagine, the standards of authority, morals and behaviour are very much lower than in earlier times. Aggressive forces always on the increase never stop their unceasing efforts to destroy. If, today, we already see much in ruins, and other landmarks disappearing all the time, it is enough to make us think of general decay in this age of tragic combat. But life goes on – yet always for the better. Things that have passed away have ceased to fulfil their functions, they were excellent in their day but were not adapted for other times.

We are at the end of one of the greatest periods in human history. Already at the end of the previous century the constituents of decay were formed and growing.

The negative destructive elements disguise themselves to look like a new society. They confuse the theories and take in ordinary people. But it is not these which will build up society which, in the immediate future, will certainly be worse than at the present time.

Only on love can a lasting society be founded. A better society can only be formed by better men. The others deceive themselves by building it up on materialism and maintaining it by violence, improving its structure without improving themselves. Only materialists and the superficial can be victims of the self-deception as they ignore the true laws of life.

The things which will take place in future years, revolts, riots, wars, and, even worse, the chaos which characterizes the present time with social conflict, the lowering of standards and rampant materialism are all part of the decay of a society which will have to be reborn, completely changed, not only in form but above all in men and in ideas.

The prophecies which are related in these pages, from

the oldest ones by Kali-yuga to the most recent prophetically inspired utterances, repeat this message with unwonted clarity. The end of this generation of Adam's descendants is described in dramatic detail. Until a short time ago many of these prophecies were not understood properly. As the age draws towards its close the warnings increase in number while relevant events occur and everything becomes clearer. Yet many people are just not aware that this is a tormented age. The same thing happened before the Flood, when men – as the Bible tells us – ate, drank and married as if everything were normal. . . . Then came the flood and everything perished.

Today the population of the world has reached the highest figure ever, three and a half billion (3,500,000,000,000). This will double at the end of the century. All the actors are taking their places on the stage for the grand finale. Because of this life today seems in confusion. But in the midst of this chaos is clear evidence of the beginnings of a new life.

The prospects for the distant future, if not the immediate future, when everything will be completed are positive in every aspect. It will be a better society of men who are more advanced spiritually and who live in a happy age because it will be based on the principle of love. Then the selfish interest of man, the desire to dominate and the appetite for sensual pleasure will give way to mutual affection, disinterested help and the pure joy of things good.

The aim is certainly very high and the road to reach it is indeed difficult.

THE DARK AGE

The progressive lowering of all standards shows the state of malaise in which we live today. In many people's minds a dark foreboding exists that things are coming to an end. They sense that this age of confusion will not continue indefinitely.

From time to time warnings are given here and there that the world is going to end very soon. But we do not mean that. Paramhansa Yogananda was once consulted by the United Press and he said that no break-up of the Earth was in sight and two billion years of ascending and descending equinoctial cycles remain to our planet in its present form. The magazine *Time* commented that this declaration was reassuring.

According to Hindu teachings, the present time is called Kaliyuga, the Dark Age, which is part of a much greater equinoctial cycle, the Manvantara. This complete cycle has lasted 25,920 years, that is terrestrial years when the sun comes back to the point when it finds itself in the spring equinox. The Manvantara is made up of four phases: Devapara-yuga, Tetra-yuga, Satya-yuga, Kali-yuga: they are like the four seasons of some great cosmic year.

Just as the life of an individual person, the life of the universe follows in alternating cycles which follow each other in the same order, following a Divine plan and regulated by laws. During these epochs, stupendous phenomena take place on earth such as the displacement of the poles which results in the movement of polar ice, the inversion of the globe and the emergence of continents with climatic differences and differing forms of the human race and civilization.

The ancient Hindu tradition has been brought to the West by means of various civilizations, Chaldean, Jewish, Egyptian and Greek. Thus Hesiod wrote of the four phases of human life: the first the Golden Age, the second the Age of Silver, the third, of Copper and the fourth of Iron, which correspond to the four points of the compass. As for the length of time they lasted, the four yugas of Manvantara, although submultiples of 25,920 are not equal in length. Thus, taking 10 to represent the complete cycle, 4 can be given to the first and longest age, 3 to the second, 2 to the third and 1 to the last and shortest. This tallies with the varying prophecies which talk of the short duration of the worst age, since the destructiveness of violent action is immediate, while creative action is more gradual.

All the prophecies agree that the phase which will succeed the present dark age, will be a happy age, the Age of Gold.

The Oldest Prophecies about the Present Time

Paramhansa Yogananda, author of the interesting book *Autobiography of a Yogi*, referring to the Hindu scriptures, confirms that the era of Kali, the Goddess of Darkness, has the worst characteristics of them all. Indeed, the fourth age, in which we are now living, in its final phases is marked by its progressively increasing materialism. The elements which make it up are quite clear to everyone who is an observer of life.

The prophecy which refers to the Kali-yuga can be read in the Vishnu Purana, one of the oldest sacred texts in India. We will quote it with a short comment. The reader will be able to see the truth of it for himself.

'The leaders who will rule over the Earth will be violent and will seize the goods of their subjects.

'The caste of servants will prevail and the outcasts will rule.

'Short will be their lives, insatiable their appetites, they will hardly understand the meaning of piety.

'Those with possessions will abandon agriculture and

16

commerce and will live as servants or following various professions.

'The leaders, with the excuses of fiscal need, will rob and despoil their subjects and take away their property.

'Moral values and the rule of law will lessen from day to day until the world will be completely perverted and agnosticism will gain the day among men.'

Man is reduced to a number, reduced from quality to quantity, and treated as one of a crowd. The proletarian classes will come to power. The proletarians, the *proles*, bodies barren in spirit and all equal like furniture castors as Guiseppe Mazzini declared.

Castes and social classes in former times had their uses because men are qualified in various ways to carry out a job according to their talents. These people knew that those who governed them with wisdom in the first age were inspired with the highest ideals. Thus the ancient races who lived out their lives under a divine king were divided into priests, brahmins; soldiers, nobles; merchants, gentlemen; lastly servants and proletarians. According to Plato, the first caste represented the spirit; the second, the mind; and the other two, the emotive feelings, activities carried out automatically, the instincts of an organic life.

The ending of every division had been brought about by love rising to the highest level of the spirit. This was the message of Jesus. It will happen in the future. On the other hand, in the Dark Age, everything is levelled down with destruction in the midst of violence.

The rising to power of inept men, sick and violent, who do not rule for the good of all on altruistic grounds but who try to impose themselves on each other and to dominate the world, has produced a hierarchy of very low standard and of intrigue. The foolish conduct of those in charge of human affairs is a reminder of what our forefathers have already written: 'God first makes mad those He wishes to destroy.'

Buddha has described the Noble Truth which does away with all pain and is made up of the eight grades of a discipline which has to be followed; right views, right thoughts, right words, right actions, a good life, right endeavours, right regard for other people and right meditation. Man has followed the opposite path, that of lies and deceit. The Westerner, extrovert and superficial, has even more stressed the race to suffering in the search for superficial comfort.

The prophecy about Kali-yuga goes on:

'The causes of devotion will be confined to physical well-being; the only bond between the sexes will be passion; the only road to success will be the lie.

'The earth will be honoured for its material treasures only.

'The priestly vestments will be a substitute for the quality of the priest.

'A simple absolution will mean purification, the race will be incapable of producing divine birth.

'Men will ask: what authority have the traditional tests?

'Marriage will cease being a rite.

'Acts of devotion, however scanty, will not produce any result.

'Every way of life will be equally promiscuous for all.'

The moral blindness will prevent many men from seeing what is the true civilization and will make them cling to their conquests which are really backward steps on the human and social paths. In this way they put a high value on atheism, divorce, strikes, the worship of their own personal comfort, indiscriminate levelling, dishonesty and sensual satisfaction. Religion, the family, work, helping other people are only taken into account if they boost that person's ego or for empty formal appearance. The things of the spirit are ignored, these things that raise Man from the animal to enable him to make contact with the superior sphere of the Invisible.

To continue:

'Those who own and spend more money will be bosses of men who will have only one aim, the gaining of wealth however dishonestly.

'Every man will consider himself as good as a brahmin.

'Men will be terrified of death and fear scarcity – by this alone will they keep up an outward appearance of religious feeling.

'Women will not obey the orders of their husbands or their parents. They will be selfish, abject, liars, fallen and given to evil ways. Their aims in life will be sensual satisfaction only.'

This extreme corruption has always come before the complete decline of a civilization. Human history offers many examples of this. The gradual sinking to the base and licentious, the work of men unable to follow the true way of life which continues to improve. It is degrading as it leads to an increasing worsening of the situation. As a result no one notices that they were being tyrannized and were submitting themselves to other forces.

Demagogues are only partly motivated by the desire to dominate others. But arrogance, based on dishonesty, makes men cowardly well before the supreme test of life, that is when it ends. Those who have not realized the difference between real values and worthless values in life often invert their values, giving greatest regard to things that are worthless. But when faced with the absolute reality of death, they are terrified. At the same time they delude themselves by practising a religion which is merely a matter of form.

As a result of the law of cause and effect, the actual final period is that when everything comes to an end. The people of the east consider the Kali-yuga the decline of the past in which all accounts are paid in the final phase. Accounts are settled so that the world can proceed into the future with a budget in the black.

This is a pleasant soothing vision and is the chief stimulus for the lives of those who have achieved spiritual maturity. As a result oriental sages have for thousands of years looked forward to what has already happened and what will happen in the years to come.

The end of the second millennium A.D. see humanity in such an excited state that all its forces are in action. The great seer Catherine Emmerich wrote:

'I have learned that Lucifer will be unchained 50 or 60 years before the year A.D. 2000.'

We see decadence today face to face unmasked in full swing on the street, in factories, offices, in public and private life, even reaching as far as the family and the schools, indeed everywhere. But above all it is in people's souls. It seems to have seeped in everywhere together with the licentiousness and the arrogance which are its characteristics. It has not even spared the church. Indeed, as we shall see later, the church thinks of heresies and schisms; and at Garabandal just as at La Salette and elsewhere the vision declares that 'Bishops will be against Bishops and Cardinals against Cardinals' and at Fatima it was clearly said 'Satan reigns in the highest places', and referring to the antipope Our Lady said 'he will succeed in penetrating to the head of the Church'.

In the book of Revelations it is written 'Woe to the inhabiters of the earth and of the sea! for the devil is come down unto you, having great wrath, because he knoweth that he hath but a short time.'

The monster advances with increasing fury. But his freedom is limited, his time is short and his power is not absolute. Until when? The Virgin Mary at San Damiano says:

'The devil is unchained now for the final conflict, but he is fearful.

'... A terrible struggle is taking place against Satan because ... the Eternal Father let him stay free ... the decisive battle is taking place between the two leaders, St. Michael and Lucifer, but, by the intervention of Him, St. Michael has received the power to crush the head of Satan and we shall have the decisive victory ... you will believe in Me ... fight by My side, with prayer, the reciting of the rosary, we shall win completely in every battle. Let us go into the attack together. The shock will be inevitable and terrible, especially for those who have no faith. Those who believe in Me, Head of the heavenly legions have nothing to fear either in life or death.' (26 May 1967).

Periods of decadence are necessary because without them life could not be imagined. They have always provided decaying material on which the new plants can develop more rigorously.

The Plan is outside Human Hands

Since 1914 humanity has lived in a period of crisis which has not occurred in any past epoch. Before this date war and revolution were comparatively local events. Since then the organization of the world has drawn together and every upheaval is felt all over the planet. The greatest advances in science and mechanics also took place then. This is confirmed in an ever in-creasing number of crises with ever-growing intensity because other factors are involved, political, economic and social. Just when a fever reveals a decaying condi-tion in the organization of the world, these have gone to confirm an increasing number of conflicts of various sorts. This phenomenon is common to everyone, a clear indication that the plan is outside human hands. Those who understand will realize without difficulty that the end of this millennium will also mark the end of a long period of civilization. Something new and exciting is being prepared for coming generations. The crisis of change is taking place now and seems to be accelerating at an increasing pace with dramatic and tragic meaning for the immediate future. All the prophecies seem to agree on this with extraordinary clarity.

2

THE ZODIAC – PISCES AND THE
AGE OF AQUARIUS

In these years we shall witness changes which would have seemed almost unthinkable to our fathers. Others we see daily with our own eyes. Utopia has become reality, dreams, concrete facts. Not only technology and science, but art, philosophy, religion and everything else will change. During the period of change there is often confusion and disorder while the old gives way to the new.

According to the astrologists the Age of Pisces is almost over, and we are about to enter the Age of Aquarius. What is about to come to an end is one of the twelve periods of time, each one 2,160 years long which make the great cosmic year.

Imagine a huge clock face, where, instead of the numerals which mark the hours, are the twelve signs of the Zodiac: Aries, Pisces, Aquarius, Capricornus, Sagittarius, Scorpio, Libra, Virgo, Leo, Cancer, Gemini, Taurus.

The turning of the hands on this clock is also to scale. Every hour corresponds to 2,160 years and the complete circuit equals 25,290 years. This period, known as a cosmic or precessional year, is the time needed for a complete revolution through the signs of the Zodiac. Stoics think that when this is accomplished there will be a universal conflagration.

Human history is marked with cycles and epochs just like the life of a man. The transition from youth to maturity at puberty and other times of change are moments of crisis. The seasons also display the phase of the year in their differing aspects. Life is changeable with a varying rhythm for every aspect. In a similar way the life of the people is carried on to a scale of centuries and that of the Earth in a scale of millennia.

Symptoms precede every change when events take place which are an advance warning and preparation for the time of change. They are always perceptible to the intelligent observer. The change is necessary to allow the work to take place. The morning light does not appear before it has conquered the darkness, the spring does not come until the winter has gone, the summit of a mountain cannot be appreciated without the stiff climb which precedes it.

The change from one sign to another is not clear-cut but slow and gradual. In a similar manner the change from night into day is not sudden, but a gradual process from dawn onwards which increases until it reaches its maximum at sunrise.

Everything which will happen in those years must be taken in relationship with the men of those times. We must believe that they will be signs which will point out the end of the preparation for the New Age. They will, on the other hand, seem even more aggressive and will take the form of even more destructive violence. The Law, in the fulfilment of its plans, will be carried on by people who of necessity, because of their own lack of development, are still on the mental level of destruction and violence; full of negativity the same mental level as the societies they have conquered using the old ways which lead to self-destruction. But this negativity will collapse first, being the worst part of the old order.

All the prophecies agree that a new order will have to replace the older order which is collapsing. And the renewal of everything will come so that life can continue. Because the New Age is coming, the old order must be eradicated, driven away, and even abolished altogether, in order to destroy the obstacle to the influx of new energy. The old will have to give way to what will come in future, as new wine cannot be put in old wineskins.

While the great clock which is The Earth is about to move its hand on the sign of Aquarius, the astrologers are not in agreement as to the exact date. Some say it will enter the age of Aquarius in 1975, others fix it at 2000, 2023 or 2160. For most people it will be changing from one outlook on life to another – more exactly men will change from seeking after knowledge to seeking after wisdom.

The events leading up to this change may not take place until 2300 according to the prophecy of Borup.

Humanity will clothe itself anew. It will be the dawn of a peaceful day after the refreshing morning bath.

The Bankruptcy of Old Myths

In the course of centuries, men have set up new ways of life in order to improve society, using first one idea and then another. But once the novelty of these ideas has worn off, these ideas collapse one by one, demonstrating their failure to bring about the improvements desired by all. This occurs because the key to all reform is neglected – the improvement of Man himself, most difficult of all, but which lasts the longest. That is why the men called politicians deceive themselves and everyone else without achieving anything positive. This has come about by social and philosophical doctrines, which are based on material facts alone and ignoring Man, without whom they would be useless.

Every theory has been publicized as well as every experiment in human history. And all have failed.

The scientific outlook of today is restricted. When the horizons have been widened and the mind raised to perceive the vision of spiritual things, Man will understand the reasons for the physical phenomena, the future of material things and the social inequality which is in the mind of Man. All harmony and contentment is the result of Man's own thoughts. But this is denied, because it is not understood, to those who have a materialistic outlook on life. Thus in our days, Marxism, the greatest inspiration of this century, deprived of these vitally necessary ideals, claims to set the ideal for Man at animal level. Marxism considers that Man has material needs only, a false and anti-scientific claim, because Man as seen by the Marxists is not a complete Man, but only the baser part at its raw and primitive state.

As an ape-like parody of an aspect of Christianity and without any real values at all, Marxism seems the real solution for many poor people and those with limited intelligence. As with all false theories it is full of deception and violence, on which is based all its power. It needs lies to gain hold on people.

The unhappy experience of previous centuries has made no impression at all on purblind men, stubborn in their mistakes, who try to build the future with the same threadbare designs.

Materialists believe that the ideals of comfort and power, gained by fighting, hate and violence can be the basis of their argument, and they forget the fact that such insecure foundations cannot be used to rule any society for long.

Collapse of the Old World

While the old world is in process of crumbling away, remaining on the defensive to keep the position which it holds despite its many mistakes, the hostile forces become more and more aggressive, using the same methods which they used in the past but which now they feel will be successful. But the forces at work today are blind, beating down everything in their way. They are destructive forces, unable to build any sort of future. Great ideals cannot come from small-minded men, they have to come from within before they can be built into the life outside.

Men can become capable of building a society truly

based on liberty, equality and fraternity only if they themselves are free and united in Spirit. This new society can only be achieved if there is a great spiritual change. The best men are beginning to realize that such a change is necessary. But in order to do this it is not necessary to look for rational formulae or purely mechanical methods because with these alone the things of the Spirit will never be achieved.

'Humanity,' many declare, 'is riding above the age when dogma, rites and priestly authority are necessary for development. But because this evolution comes peacefully it is necessary that Man will first learn that self-discipline which is more important than external things to inspire and guide Man on the road to Life.'

Now is the Time of Chaos

We seem in reality to be under a double influence, both of a sign that is coming to an end and another which is starting; and this explains the contrast, contradictions and contests of our times. This is the age in which hooligans mix with saints, scoundrels with idealists, delinquents with holy men. Now is the time of chaos.

When each sign of the Zodiac comes to the end of its time, disorder and chaos take place. This is why we are going through such stormy times. The forces of good and evil are in conflict. From a period of confusion, signs of a new life movement will arise which will bear the marks of a new age.

There are those who say that we are already influenced by Aquarius. The influence of the new sign was made felt at the end of the last century and has begun to show itself in scientific discovery. The invention of the steam engine in 1698 was the dawn of the advancing new age. Then in a growing crescendo came the other inventions which have revolutionized the customs of an epoch.

By natural law of the fall of a body, the velocity increases towards the end. *Motus in fine velocior*. The movement of acceleration is getting faster all the time as the fall grows near. In the age in which we live today time seems to have altered its value. Problems which once took years to solve now work themselves out in weeks. Events take place at ever-increasing speed.

The actual great moment of humanity is very clearly shown by the furthest point Man has reached in scientific discovery. The splitting of the atom, the escape from the gravity of the Earth, are facts which are out of proportion to the moral stature of Man today, as he is still selfish. He is not convinced that he sees before him the fatal choice, complete destruction or rising to the higher spiritual levels. Surrounded by such enormous forces, Man cannot remain a moral pygmy.

Inspiration for the New Life

That life cannot go on advancing at this rate as it is today for very much longer is clear from everything that has been said so far. The feeling that it is temporary, expressed by the transitoriness and the effort of all human work in every field, is felt everywhere. It is a warning of a breaking limit which if exceeded will cause a general collapse which cannot be remedied.

The inspiration of the new life can be felt not only inside every man but in his surroundings and in society. The struggles, the revolts, the collisions are the tumult of a dying world and the seed of something new which is about to be born.

Many men are looking for something new, want other ways of protecting life, are taken in by old things and cling tenaciously to each other. Meanwhile everyone is agitated just as is a ship by the waves before the anchor is sent down.

The principles on which the new society will have to be founded are already to be found in the hearts of many people. If they are almost lacking in some people, others have them more clearly. They are the same principles which were betrayed by the egotism of the past by immature men still incapable of putting them into action.

The tendency towards planetary unity is shown by the hopes of much vaster regroupings. There is a feeling of dissatisfaction with limiting frontiers, national and provincial. Less than a century of technical inventions has been enough to break down many barriers already. The speeding up of communications and of news has already created the promise of that much greater unity which will create the New Era.

Humanity is starting towards a truer unity, that of the mind full of peace and love. All work is beneficial. Praise the hard work which will produce it.

The Crisis of Transition

'Today we are living in a world of transition. The ancient Gods must fall before the new altars are ready, the fighting of the sparrows will be stopped and they will be invited to eat elsewhere. Fear has died too soon before the dignity of man has adapted itself to indulge in fewer fantasies, which horrible thing comes from rationalist fanatics and crowds of demagogues.' These are the words of Paolo Mantegazza, extraordinarily apt today. The chaos of today is the result of this and many other causes which are now coming to fruition as well as the instability of things when changing.

The present years, as well as those in the future, are years when all values are questioned, because they belong neither to the previous cycle of years nor to those which will follow, but which come between the end of one epoch and the start of the other. They destroy external authority before self-discipline is born inside man.

The End of the Age of Pisces

The Greek word *ichthys* means fish. The early Christians used the fish as the symbol of Christ. The letters making the word 'ΙΧΘΥΣ (ichthys) were the initials of the phrase 'Ιησυς Χριστος θεου Υίος Σωτηρ (Jesus Christ, Son of God (and) Saviour).

About two thousand years ago Jesus was born on Earth and was the spiritual impulse of what was then the New Age, the Christian Era. Today we are at the end of that epoch. A glance will show that man during these twenty centuries is really little different now from what he was then. Evolution in spiral form has caused man to rise even higher after an apparent setback. It will carry him to a higher level of understanding.

For millions of people the Light of Christ has not been wasted in illuminating the world as they have achieved sublime heights both by that light and by the impetus given by Christ to human evolution. Great events will take place while humanity prepares for another great leap up towards the true life.

Towards a New World

A society of people divided against each other in a continual struggle will not be able to live peacefully together owing to egotism, self-interest or pride. These inferior stages of evolution are being overcome. Jesus preached Love, realizing very well that it is the sole means of salvation for those who need other men for survival and for progress.

Humanity, in ferment of evolution, looks for this new way. After being bathed in destructive materialism, it will rediscover spiritual values, the only ones which will support a lasting cilivization. Darkness always comes before any dawn. But the Light always comes in the end. When every other system has failed the only thing remaining is the Gospel of Love, the only valid and unique road to salvation for a humanity drifting aimlessly, the only way which can lead humanity to the fulfilment of all its aspirations. The Christian seed, thrown on the ground two thousand years ago, has sprouted only today after deceptions which have proved false. After a long gestation the seed will sprout, the plant will grow and bear its fruits.

By this we do believe that the future society will be truly Christian, that is to say the religion of Love, not the version we have had hitherto. This is a superficial Christianity, as inside the people remained pagan, which was a continuation of Judaism. If man continues to fight, to hate and to overpower each other as before, only the name and the label of the religion will have changed.

The Age of Aquarius

After traversing the sign of Pisces, Humanity will enter Aquarius which has different characteristics from the time that has gone by. Everything will be changed as it will be another era in the history of Man. It presents itself as the vision of a renewed Humanity. Society will not be based on self-interest, not on possessions which are always the cause of fighting and furious feuds. Aquarius is a sign of reform in the field of human thought. Thus it will be a time of tolerance between all the religions which previously presented the not very edifying spectacle of controversy and indeed bloodshed between them.

The extraordinary developments in science which have revolutionized the way Man thinks and lives when he is not prepared for them spiritually, can be considered manifestations which anticipate what society will be like in the future. Indeed, according to the studies of astrology, Aquarius has the face of a lion, symbolizing force and domination, which announces an age not only of peace but of great scientific discoveries in every field and of social advances useful to humanity. Every brand of the sciences, medicine, surgery, transport will be more advanced in future thanks to the work of men who are knowledgeable and intelligent. In the social field the principles of justice and love will be fully applied, proclaimed today but only partially applied.

Man will increase his sense of intuition and this will be the normal way of learning as he makes gradual progress.

The application of rights will not be for selfish use as it is in the present society, which is under-developed morally, but with the justice of a man who is quite balanced having overcome his lower feelings.

Aquarius is the symbol of renaissance. The millennia to come, after the storm which will purify both men and things, will truly be a new life for men of good will.

The Age of Aquarius is that about which Jesus says: 'But the hour cometh, and now is, when the true worshippers shall worship the Father in spirit and in truth: for the Father seeketh such to worship him. God is a Spirit: and they that worship him must worship him in spirit and in truth.' (John 4 : 23–4.)

Every symbol of the Divine Being will be banned. Everything that for two thousand years has been the cause of competition and divisions, Churches, possessions, stipends, buying power and followers, temporal authority, belong to a past of men yet unprepared for the realization of higher things. Temples and altars will not be made of stone and statues, but in the heart of man alone. Judaism will be clearly overcome by the affirmation of the authentic Christianity of love.

It will be confirmed that Christ has come to all those who understand the meaning of love. It is, indeed, essential for the new world, it will be the basis of love between men, that which is called brotherly as all are sons of the Father, who works together for the same family.

In the new solar cycle of the sign of Aquarius Christ will be the 'Giver of the Water of Life.'

'Whosoever drinketh of this water shall thirst again: but whosoever drinketh of the water that I shall give him shall never thirst; but the water that I shall give him shall be in him a well of water springing up into everlasting life.' (John 4 : 13–14.)

3

1000 AND NOT MORE THAN 1000

The origin of the huge mistake which threw Europe into confusion at the end of the year 1000 seems to have been a mistaken interpretation of the Bible. The text which is referred to declares that a thousand happy years will begin after the troubles Mankind has been through during the scourge of those years.

'Appropinquante mundi termine' – the end of the world draws near – is the formula which is found in many deeds relating to donations to monasteries, churches, societies of brothers, with which wills, private documents begin in the Middle Ages, as if they understood that the beneficiaries would receive these good things if the world has not yet come to an end. The phenomenon was first seen at the end of 534 and occurred with increasing frequency towards the year 1000. But absolutely nothing happened. The fear came back little by little as the year 1100 drew near. When that date passed the folly began again about the year 1200. Chiara di Assissi was witness to other scares in 1245.

Thus from century to century during all the Middle Ages this terror remained in the hearts of most people, increased by false seers, astrologers and preachers whose false prophecies added to the foolish confusion. Until finally the Vth Lateran Council forbade the discussion of the immediate end of the world.

At the end of this Millennium by an odd reversal of feeling, we see the foolish agitation about another illusion, that of the Sun of the Future. From the terror of being raised to Heaven to the fanaticism of the masses – these are two meaningless movements, based on unreality. But folly is like water which takes the shape of the vase which holds it.

It was believed for centuries that the age of the Earth from the creation of the world, was 6,000 years. We can cite the Talmud, St. Augustine (*De Civitate Dei*, book 20 chapter 7), St. Jerome (Explanation of Psalm 29 in *Ad Appianum*). All the learned men from the past repeated this mistake. This calculation followed the others, it was repeated by the ancient fathers of the church and not refuted or explained by learned theologians that the world would last for six thousand years and no longer than that.

The ancient tradition derives from the first book of the Bible, Genesis, where it is written 'And on the seventh day God rested,' this was interpreted by the Epistle of St. Barnabas, not accepted as canonical scripture, which says 'In six days, that is in six thousand years, the Universe will come to an end.' St. Hilary comments 'Just as the world was made in six days, it will come to an end in six thousand years.' (*Haeres*, book 8.) Those who worked it out in the Jewish usage thought there were 4,000 years before the birth of Christ and 2,000 years of the Christian era. The sixth millennium will be completed at the end of this century and therefore we should be entering the seventh millennium. In the second Epistle of St. Peter it is written that to God 'a thousand years are as one day'. The life of the Adamite generation has thus been worked out by many people as 6,000 years, divided into six Biblical days of 1,000 years each.

But today things are viewed in a very different perspective. The age of the Earth has been calculated to about 4,000,000,000,000 years and it has been proved that Man has lived on this grain of sand circling in space for millions of years. In this period of time civilizations have followed one another in untold numbers. 6,000 years are only a small part of the amount of time Man has spent on the Earth.

The age of the Earth is confused with the length of

the Adamic generations and the error of this extraordinary interpretation has been carried on until comparatively recent times. From that arose other errors which were sources of misunderstandings. All the Biblical commentators, among them Nostradamus, calculated in the same way. Among those who measured the duration of the world in seven eras, after the days of creation, were men who were eminent in every field.

The current universal belief is that at the end of this century we shall come to an end of the sixth millennium and start the seventh. It will not be the end of the world but only the end of the generation of Adam. This is what Jesus is referring to in the Gospel when he said 'This generation shall not pass away until My words have been fulfilled.' At the time of St. Paul this error had already been made and even then everyone was awaiting the end.

Is it only now as we come to the end of this century, that this generation which has lasted so long is indeed coming to the end of its time?

The Idea of the Millennium lives on

The views of the Millenarists are very old and were also supported by the Church fathers. They thought that Jesus Christ would reign openly on Earth for 1,000 years with the Saints until the end of that time when there would be a general resurrection. They were also called Chiliasti from the Greek word which meant 1,000.

These people taught that at the first resurrection those that would take part in it would be the just only, thus they would be the only ones to take part in the thousand happy years. Taking everything literally, many of them declared that Jerusalem and the Temple would be rebuilt with new splendour. There were those even who could describe in advance the happiness which would be enjoyed in this new reign. Those who were alive when the thousandth year came would preserve their lives, the good to obey the risen just ones and the bad to be their slaves. Christ would then be seen in the Heavens.

When the reign of the Millennium is over, the Devil would attack the saints of Judea, dragging with them people who were called those of Gog and Magog. A tornado of flame would destroy the unfaithful. Then the general resurrection would take place. At this second resurrection, reserved for those who had not passed the test of the first one, universal justice would take place with the punishment of some and the rewarding of others, punishment and pleasure which some took to be spiritual and some took to be carnal.

Even today the idea of the Millennium survives in a number of different religions and creeds. In America the doctrine of the Mormons preaches the reality of the idea of the Millennium. The same teaching is found with the Jehovah's Witnesses, spread throughout the world, who preach it as a certainty. In their writings and publications they say that entry into the seventh Millennium is imminent, in which all will be peace and good-will between men.

It seems that the idea of the Millennium lives on, therefore it can be accepted as a view that will never be out-dated.

And the End of the World?

The people who believed in Millenarism in the past have made a mistake about the time of the Millennium and nothing else. 'A thousand and not another thousand' does not refer to the year 100 but to today. That is the opinion of those who are convinced that the first thousand years after Christ have gone by but not the other thousand. The well-known saying could well refer to our own times. We have almost witnessed the completion of 'and not another thousand'.

Remember, too, that Garabandal declared to Conchita Gonzales 'It is the end of time but not the end of the world.' A well-known seer Antony Gay (1790–1871)

35

cried 'the thing that concerns me is the thought that the end of time is coming and we shall be able to do no more evil . . . Satan is on the Earth for some time, the Earth has changed its appearance from the time that he was unchained, disorder, terror and impiety increase daily . . . at the end of time there will be signs of all types . . . note well . . . their precursors can already be seen.'

On a question of this sort the views of the Popes cannot be neglected. The authority which at one time refuted Millenarism, today proclaims it all the time. Times have changed and many things will soon come to maturity. What the Popes wrote on this subject is very clear.

Pius X, the holy Pope, who saw Antichrist in the atheist and pagan society of his day wrote thus about the disbelief of the Nations: 'Those who value these things have the right to fear that such a spiritual perversion is the beginning of the evil announced for the end of time and almost their contact with the Earth that the son of perdition which is mentioned by the Apostles are already here among us now.'

Benedict XV, on 1 November 1914 announced in his encyclical that the 1914–18 war was the beginning of the last age: 'the beginning of the sadness and the agony of the world'. Words with a clear meaning, almost the words of a prophet.

Pius XI in the encyclical *Caritate Dei* wrote 'After the flood we were faced with a difficult crisis, both spiritual and mental which went very deep like that which we are going through now.' In another encyclical *Miserrimus Redemptor* he defined this comparison even better: 'We are not able to avoid thinking that these are really the signs of the last age as was announced by Our Lord.'

Pius XII declared in 1947: 'Today the spirit of evil has been unchained with such bitterness in order to predict a decisive solution if it did not know that it would last a long time for most of the world and that it would end with the victory of God.'

The words and deeds of John XXIII and Paul VI have

strengthened the view even more that the thought of the Popes on this subject is clearly directed towards this knowledge. And their actions in recent years show that they know more than they say.

St. Hildegarde wrote that the voice of Heaven has revealed that all who live on the Earth are destined to perish, that the Earth itself can feel the weakening forces; the cataclysms which convulse it will bring its present existence to an end. She tells us that we are in the period which comes before the seventh day.

But it is an ending coming before the start of a new cycle of events. It is the opinion of many that we are living today in times which the Book of Revelations calls apostasy, rebellions and Antichrist which is typical of the Last Hour. After that comes the end.

The natural desire to find out moves the people to inquire and to ask 'When will all this happen?'

GIOACCHINO DA FIORE AND THE AGE OF THE SPIRIT

Gioacchino da Fiore was an austere Cistercian monk, a reformer in his community and was inspired to make his own community like the hermitages of Tebaide which he had visited. He lived from 1130 until 1202 in Calabria, where he was born and where he later became abbot of the monastery of Corazza. He wrote books on the prophecies of Sibilla Eritrea, the prophecies of Merlin, he commented on the Biblical prophets and on the Book of Revelation, but his most famous work was the *Vaticini del Vangelo eterno* (Prophecies of the Eternal Gospels).

He was the inspiration for a new and growing age and, as in a prophetic vision, he sensed the cosmic preparation for great events. His work about the prophecies was printed for the first time about 1484, but without date or place. Many editions were printed of this book, some of them with Italian text as well as Latin. In others, the prophecies credited to Anselm, Bishop of Marsico, were added and symbols, figures with wheels, images, and Arabic and Turkish inscriptions were reproduced.

Dante believed in Gioacchino and, just as with St. Francis of Assissi, was inspired by him. He meets him in Paradise (Par, XII) and makes St. Bernard say of him:

> He illuminates me from the flank
> The Calabrian abbot Gioacchino
> Whose spirit has the power of prophecy.

The Prophecies of Abbot Gioacchino

He announced the coming of a new Church of the Holy Spirit, after the age of the Father and of the Son.

His teaching was that the world has three ages, the first that of the Old Testament, that is the age of the Father, the law and fear; the second, the New Testament, the age of the Son and of faith; the third, the age of the Holy Spirit, of mutual love, of peace. He expected this final age to begin about 1260.

The third age, according to Gioacchino, will be preceded by persecutions and calamities after which the ETERNAL GOSPEL will be proclaimed. The whole constitution of the church will be transformed and the spiritual interpretation of the Gospels will be realized.

'Peter will disappear in front of John, because the reign of the Holy Spirit will be the reign of the free.

'In the first world epoch were slaves, in the second, free men, in the third, communities of friends. In the first, law will dominate, in the second, grace, and in the third, a fuller and more generous grace. In the first epoch; servile slavery, whipping, domination of the old, winter, etc.; in the second: wisdom, progeny, light of dawn, spring, shoots of corn and vine, children; in the third: beginning of real liberty, contemplation, charity, friends, shade, summer, corn, oil, Easter of resurrection.'

A New Church when the Present One is Abolished

For Gioacchino, the Church of Symbols had to be succeeded by the Church of Spiritual Realism.

Always an innovator of concessions, but with deference and a feeling of veneration towards the Church, Gioacchino da Fiore said that just as symbols always give way to reality as 'the hierarchical church will always give way to the Church of the Spirit when the hour strikes. Everything in this is a symbol of temporariness. We cannot, however, give up former traditions which have a virtue of their own.'

The third period which was about to begin, would differ from that which had gone before: 'in disinterestedness and in humility they will proclaim as the only law, that of the spirit, love'. The intensity of the cultural and theological life of the Latin Church is 'only a pale and wan prologue of the coming revelation of the Holy Spirit'.

These theories would have many followers and would spread in the main in mystic fields and have many interpretations. They had a notable influence on Dante and many of his followers. Some of them took the prophecies as referring to their own times, although Gioacchino referred to his age. And in the works of later writers they began to take on all sorts of distortions. The Franciscans, above all, postponed the time of these prophecies as if they referred to their own order. But they did not delay in taking other routes, taking part in the life of their day, taking part in the conflicts of their time, mixing them up with polemics which had been launched against the Inquisition.

Gioacchino da Fiore, in his day held that the end would be soon.

'With the year 1201, in the pontificate of Innocent III, the 42nd generation. It was necessary to raise the heart in hope.

'This Order which, owing to the brilliance of its knowledge could then be defined in golden terms has darkened until today it is once more murky and leaden. And those who resembled precious jewels and were incarcerated in solitary cloisters of the heart are today spread out in the long streets and in the corners of the noisy squares, intent on disposing of external affairs and on dismissing controversies which were not good. To the expiation of the blows of the Church itself, those who occupied the priestly succession, did nothing to make themselves like spiritual men, but concentrated on the things of this world and in seeking material advantages for themselves.'

This might well be describing ecclesiastic custom in our own day! Gioacchino also declares that the epoch of the VIth Angel of the Apocalypse has already begun and is destined to come to an end with all speed and urgency.

With the thought of Gioacchino as their doctrine were founded the movements of the Flagellants, the Spirituals, the Fraticelli and the Beghini with their obvious exaggerations and deviations.

The direct or indirect influence of Gioacchino da Fiore is seen in the prophecies of Savonarola, in the philosophy of G. B. Vico, in the aspirations of Cola di Rienzo and even in Mazzini and in the poet Ibsen. Arguments of Gioacchino were also taken over by St. Bonaventura and St. Bernard of Siena. Today, those who do not accept the old structure and even more, feel the need for renovation in the Church in the spiritual sense, repeat his thoughts.

The great vision of the future and the affirmation of spiritual values on Earth is the true meaning of the message of Gioacchino da Fiore. Their reality is in the desire for a spiritual revival, felt more than ever in this age.

The presupposition of his faith as with all those who today expect an imminent and drastic change in the life of men was and is the certainty of a divine plan in nature and in history which would follow and be carried on in similar cycles. We do not know why his ideas were condemned. It was not possible for the Seer himself to know anything about it; he had been dead ten years when Innocent III in the Lateran Council of 1212 rejected his theories.

The Age of the Spirit

The Third Age of Gioacchino da Fiore will recognize in full the truth mysteriously conceived in the New Testament.

The beginning of the new cycle, according to him, as also with the Hindu tradition, will have to be preceded by disaster, then to solidify in an era of peace and love. In this most significant similarity, the ancient and recent traditions come together and the message is proclaimed, as well by the prophecies which we are going to look at in turn.

According to Gioacchino, the Third Age will be perfect

and conclusive just as if the Holy Spirit, preceded by the Father and the Son, closed the circle of the Trinity. The Third Age will mark the coming of love which will destroy every advance of grovelling fear and any interference of authority between God and His Son, and it will be the Age of Perfection.

One can almost hear the echo of these words in the affirmation of S. Louis M. Grignion of Monfort who wrote: 'The special reign of God the Father has lasted from the Flood and will end with a superabundance of water, the reign of Jesus Christ ended with a surge of blood, but the Reign of the Holy Spirit will end with a flood of fire, love and justice.'

In her *Life of the Saint of Coutances*, Marie de Vallées wrote: 'There are three floods, all three of them sad, sent to destroy sin. The first flood is that of the Eternal Father; it was a flood of water; the second is that of the Son: it was a flood of blood; the third is that of the Holy Spirit: it will be a flood of fire. But it will be sad like the others, because it will come up against much resistance and a large amount of green wood, difficult to burn. Two of them have taken place, but the third is yet to come; and as the first two were predicted a long time in advance, the same is true of the last one, of which God Himself alone at the present time knows the date.'

5

ATLANTIS – THE PROPHECY OF THE GREAT PYRAMID

All religions seem to preserve the memory of a primitive paradise, called Eden in the Bible, from which many people believe our fathers came and whose gates were guarded by an angel with a flaming sword. Many people think that Atlantis could have been that happy place of delight.

A Civilization which has Disappeared

A million years ago, the appearance of the Earth was not the same as it is today, and the seas were located in different places from on a modern map. Most of the Earth was then covered by water, and what is now dry land was then under the waves, leaving parts uncovered here and there: they were the islands which we are going to explore. For the Hyperborean, Lemurian, Poseidonian and Atlantean peoples had to live on summits of these subterranean mountains.

If the ice in Antartica were melted, the level of the oceans would rise about fifty metres. If this happened, cities with a population of several millions, such as London, Paris, Rome, New York and many others would be covered by water. This depressing hypothesis has not come to pass because it is a physical impossibility.

In the passing of epochs upon Earth, civilizations fell and others arose. Bertrand Russell said that of twenty-one past civilizations, of which we only know the names of a few and then only the names, another fourteen disappeared after having left the barest minimum trace.

Plato mentions Atlantis in *Crisis* and *Timeus*. Plutarch wrote about it as well as Diderus Siculus, Strabo, Macrobius, Elianus and Proclus. This last writer mentions seven islands, perhaps the Canaries, sacred to Proserpina and three others sacred to Pluto, the sun god Ammon and to Poseidon.

After having reached a high level of civilization in which scientific knowledge seemed to have reached a very high level, equal to, if not better than that of today, degeneration set in and decadence of the inhabitants. The people abused for their own ends the knowledge and the technical application and the same way that we can see ourselves doing with our own eyes today.

The submersion of Atlantis by means of monstrous cataclysms did not come at once but gradually during the course of many millennnia during which the Earth underwent radical changes. Successive catastrophies completed the work of the complete renewal of the planet.

In this way Atlantis, Isle of the Saturns, kingdom of bronze and brass where the cult of the Sun was born and flourished, disappeared for ever.

Atlantis and the Pyramids

Thousands of millions of years are, for the life of the Earth, the equivalent of a few days in our own life. W. Scott-Elliot in the *Story of Atlantis* declares that about two hundred thousand years ago, an empire was founded in which reigned the first Divine Dynasty in Egypt.

'In this period the first large contingent of colonists arrived from Atlantis and in the space of time before the second catastrophe lasting about ten thousand years, the two Great Pyramids of Ghizeh were built to prepare the rooms given over to the initiation rites and partly to hide some of the powerful talismans which were used for domination during the cosmic cataclysms foreseen by the Initiates.'

But Egypt, too, was submerged and remained under the water for a considerable time.

'When it emerged once more,' continued W. Scott-Elliot, 'it was repopulated with the descendants of the original inhabitants who had taken refuge in the mountains of Abyssinia, new Atlantean colonists came in from every part of the world, and a considerable immigration of Akkadians contributed a lot to modify the Egyptian race. In this period of time the epoch of the second Divine Dynasty of Egypt began; the Alchemists who were the Initiates ruled the countryside once more.'

The catastrophe which took place about eight thousand years ago, was a second submersion of the country, which however, did not last very long. When the water subsided the 'third divine dynasty' mentioned by Manetho, took control and it was under the rule of these first kings of this dynasty that the great temple of Karnak and other buildings were put up whose ruins we can see today. Indeed, no buildings in Egypt are earlier than the catastrophe of eight thousand years ago except the two pyramids.

The final submersion of Poseidon caused a third flooding of Egypt which was of very short duration, and caused the end of the Divine Dynasties as the Lodge of the Initiates transferred their seat elsewhere.

Thus, therefore, Atlantis and the Pyramids seemed to have a bond. Nothing can be added to those historical documents. The memory of man is too weak, memory in the sense, too, of writings and witnesses when faced with the destructive action of time. But, perhaps, the best way to do it was to inscribe records on something which cataclysms could not destroy – in stone and in an enormous building. And this is all that remains.

The Secret of the Pyramid of Cheops

In front of the Pyramids is the Sphinx, as a guard, as if to call attention to the fact that it contains a message for Man in times to come and for the future of the world.

The English mathematician John Taylor declared in 1850 that the Great Pyramid contained a divine revelation or a prophecy. He discovered the unit of measurement used to build the Pyramids, the Polar inch. An Arab writer of the tenth century, Masoudi, had already written,

'Surid, one of the kings of Egypt before the great flood, had had the two largest pyramids built and ordered the priests to store away carefully the written records of their wisdom and of their knowledge in artistic and scientific fields as well as the names and ownership of plants used in medicine and everything to do with arithmetic and geometry. Last of all, the kings deposited in the Pyramid indications of the position of the stars and their movement across the skies, the history and the chronicles of times past and prophecies of things to come.'

The Pyramids were certainly built by the ancient Initiates with the collaboration of architects, priests, astrologers in which were united the knowledge of mathematics, astronomy and the desire to hand on their mysterious messages to future generations with a symbolic form of building which would only be understood at the end of time. The mysterious science of the Pharaohs was not going to be lost to Man.

Situated at the apex of the Nile Delta near Cairo, the Pyramid of Cheops is larger than any of the others. It is 137 metres high with bases of 227 metres each orientated with geometric precision so that the entrance faces due north. This imposing work of Man, if an empty shell, is large enough to contain inside itself the great Basilica of St. Peter in Rome.

To build this pyramid about 2,600,000 square metres of limestone whose weight was 6,500,000 metric tons were needed. According to Herodotus, the construction lasted twenty years with the help of enormous efforts on the part of numberless slaves.

Historians repeat the normal interpretation of the internal passages, which in many ways seem incomplete. Against the interpretation which is often funereal can be set features which can have no other explanation than symbolic and prophetic. There is another explanation which gives the enormous pile of stones a religious significance to this colossal construction. If anyone knows how to interpret it, the pryamidologists declare,

46

in the Pyramid of Cheops are to be found the most important dates in the history of Humanity.

The ancient Egyptians used the cubit for measurement, and later on the Hebrews used the same unit in the building of the Temple of Solomon and for the making of the Ark. The sacred cubit was used by the Initiates while everyone else did their calculations in ordinary cubits. They were also called pyramidical cubits and consisted of 25 pyramidical inches. Inches and cubits correspond to the two standard weights, according to which, Davidson declared, the searchers into the future would have to measure the architectural apocalypse. To the pyramidical inch, in the measurement of time, the value of one solar year was given.

The Meaning of the Esoteric Symbols

The symbol has always been used by Man. The ordinary man measures the surface of things and uses symbols to record them. But underneath they are something more, what we call substance. Even the age of materialism wishes to forget Latin and only keep the outward trimmings of the language.

The Sphinx seems to summarize and record the many thousands of years of human evolution, the road which man, then still half animal, has had to take to reach divinity. The four principal signs of the Zodiac, Taurus, Leo, Scorpio and Aquarius, symbols, too, of the four Evangelists, show the starting point and the halfway mark from the ground to the sky; from some crawling to having wings, from the Earth to the sky and from Man to God.

From the splendid scientific and esoteric knowledge, which includes facts like the distance from the Earth to the Sun, the length of the circumference of the Earth, causes the Pyramid to be called 'The Bible in Stone'.

Even the form of the Pyramids themselves indicates, in its symbolism, the evolutionary tendency to evolve from multiplicity to one. In its esoteric meaning the

47

square base and the triangular sides indicate respectively the four ages of matter, birth, development, maturity, death; which are fulfilled in the three aspects of the spirit, mind, soul, love. A four-fold law for the four ages of Humanity and in the life of a man. A three-fold law for the three-fold sphere of the spirit. At the top, all are reunited in the Superior Mind of the Creator: God. The 4 and 3 together make 7, which is well-known as a symbolic number in all religions.

In the Pyramid itself the stone at the top is missing, the symbol which indicates Christ. Jesus said to his disciples 'Did ye never read the Scriptures, The stone which the builders rejected, the same is become the head of the corner: this is the Lord's doing and is marvellous in our eyes!' (Matthew 21 : 42.)

It has been justly observed that the Pyramid is not complete without that stone as angle, headstone and cuspid. Christ has referred to Himself as the Cornerstone. Only his coming can complete the building. The 'Lord of the Pyramid' is the Messiah waited for by all the people for millennia.

The Prophetic Message of the Great Pyramid

Many Arab writers confirm the symbolism of the Great Pyramid. In its internal passages, the corridors, the rooms, the steps, the passages and the little passages would represent the measurement of time and the phases in the history of Humanity until 'the end of time'. This prophecy is not written on parchment, but engraved in the massive stone walls which resist the vicissitudes of the millennia. The message can thus be transmitted to generations to come with complete certainty of overcoming any risks from human frailty.

Is the Future of Humanity written in the Pyramids?

Robert Menzies in 1865 was the first to put forward the hypothesis that the internal passages formed a chronological outline of the prophecies, and the unit of calculation in this chronological scale was the inch, and above all, that the Grand Gallery symbolized the Christian era by its shape, height and length.

The point about which the interpreters disagree is in calculating the beginning of the Christian era, some make it begin at the birth of Jesus Christ, others at His death.

The Dates and the Events

According to Habermann, the Pyramids recount the Adamic epoch to its final end in its architectural, historical and scientific dates. Thus it has a calendar in stone taking in six thousand years, the whole Adamic era which began in the year 4000 B.C.

It is very important to point out that Christ is the central figure in the whole of human history. The search for a Messiah is not a phenomenon confined to the Hebrew people. It was the hope of every individual person and the hope of all races. The Pyramids had, therefore, a value which was, above all, messianical because the prophetic dates in it went on until the end of the Christian era (2001, or, according to others, 2090).

The calculations are made by translating the dates and interpreting the internal passages, by means of complicated operations, with astronomical and geometric dates. According to these calculations the year 0 is under the level of the pyramid in the point of axis of the Corridor which descends, in perfect proportion, where it crosses the line of the original limestone covering of the edge of the Pyramid, also in perfect proportion under the surface.

A Journey inside the Pyramid

Entering the huge edifice, crossing the entrance gate as far as the sixteenth row one begins to go down towards the depths. The passages which rise have the symbolic meaning of improvement, progress, and seeking the light, while those which go down stand for degeneration and setbacks, therefore this period is shown to be an epoch of spiritual degeneration.

Continuing the journey one goes along the entrance corridor, which in the symbolism of the stone indicates times of preparation, then comes a narrow section which means an epoch of poverty. There is even a room where men are shown walking upside down, indicating the folly of men who see everything in reverse.

The system of corridors, stairs, galleries, storeys, passages, ante-chambers has its own language. The measurement is made with great accuracy of geometrical data. Even the orientation of the entrances and the rooms has its own symbolic character.

The Christian Era

When going through the internal passages one reaches the threshold of the Grand Gallery which the Egyptian texts call 'The Passage of the Pure Waters of Life', the Christian Era begins. And the period begins on 7 April 30 according to the Julian Calendar. The height, the inclination and the length of the Grand Gallery have been accurately measured, valued and interpreted by students for the great importance of that period.

The length of the Grand Gallery is 153 feet, the number of the fishes in the Gospel, at the ceiling, or 1,836 inches, while at ground level it is 157 feet or 1,884⅓ inches, and ends with the Grand Staircase. The number 153 is equal to the number of fishes caught by the Apostles when ordered to do so by the Risen Christ. (John 21 : 1–14.)

The narrative is filled with details that seem unnecessary, of that miraculous fishing trip on the Sea of Galilee which would seem irrelevant if we did not know that the fact was taken from ancient symbolism of the whole of the Christian story. In the account in the Gospel, when mentioning what was in the boat and how they nearly foundered as a result of their heavy load, the phrase 'they were not far from land, but as it were, two hundred cubits' is very notable.

Now, G. Barberin observes, we have taken these dates, if we add the number 1,884⅓ (in a scale of one inch per year) to 7 April 30, date of the death of Jesus Christ and the true beginning of the Christian Era, we get the date 4–5 August 1914, a date of great importance in the prophetic geometry of the Pyramid. Indeed, according to the interpretation of many people, this date of 1914 corresponds to the Great Staircase, retaining an essential character of all the prophecies of the pyramid.

Our own Times...

The Grand Staircase exists at the end of the rising corridor. The date corresponding to it, 1914, represents the beginning of our troublous years, in view of the 'consummation of time' in biblical language, and of the 'reconstruction of everything' according to the key in the Book of the Dead of Egypt.

From the top of the Grand Staircase the progress of Humanity becomes precipitous as the unity of measurement, the inch, is given no more than thirty days in value by some students, rather than a solar year. With this measurement the journey through the Pyramid reaches 2001. Other interpretations give the same value to the inch all through the passage, also after the Grand Staircase. In this case all the chronology has to be changed and the last date becomes 2444.

G. Barberin writes 'After passing the Grand Staircase, Humanity does not advance any further with its spiritual growth, but on the horizontal plane. It enters now into the Epoch of Chaos in which it has to proceed by curves through the Lower Corridors with an interruption in the ante-room before reaching the Hall of the King.'

The turnings which began with this date can be extended, according to some pyramidologists, until 2030, the date which marks the end of the message of the pyramids. Others think that it goes on for some years after that. Rudolf Werner in his book *The Secret of the Pyramid of Cheops* says that the transformation from our epoch to the new era will take place between 2013 and 2090.

The Grand Staircase is the start of the preparations for the end which is in sight. Indeed, from 1914–18, the dates of the First World War, humanity has taken on another aspect and another rhythm. Without entering too much into details of facts and dates, which we could not guarantee for certain in any case, we will outline the interpretations of noted pyramidologists such as David-son, who G. Barberin relates in his book *The Prophecies of the Great Pyramid or the End of the Adamic World*.

Davidson affirms that after calculations and measur-ing the distance of the second corridor, he found a strange similarity and analogy to the dates and measures with the architectural section which announced the birth of Jesus. From this he formed the hypothesis that in October 1936 the human Antichrist would be born. It would be, thenceforward, a time of confusion. In such a time – that of destruction – the people would root out the bases of past civilizations.

In the prophetic topography of the Pyramids the epochs seem to be accurate but not the individual years, as the dates are things of man while the phases which follow one another are the design of the work which comprises them.

... And Future Time

The King's Chamber comes after the Grand Staircase. This is also called 'Hall of Justice and of the Purification of the Nations', and 'The Return of the Pure Light, which comes from the West', and added to this chamber are two passages and an ante-room.

The first low passage indicates the period of chaos; the ante-room the truce in the chaos and the second low passage the final humiliation which will be succeeded by the new Light, the Hall of Kings.

From 1914 other salient facts have been the Second World War (1939–45) which certainly resulted from the situation which had been created in Europe from 1935–6. Indeed, in the symbology of the Pyramid, all dates from September 1936 changed its direction once more from the first time since the entrance corridor.

Other notable dates which the Pyramids are believed project are 1953 and 1966. The last date is that of December 1992. Dates of less importance are also given. Great events to be expected in the future years are: the coming of the Grand Monarch who will be in command until the last days when the order of things will be convulsed by the hammer and sickle, then the form Antichrist takes, and the second coming of Christ.

The facts will have to be verified as the years roll by, especially those which separate the years 2030 and 2090 according to the most usual explanation. Other people believe that these dates may well be wrong.

But lastly, after so much sadness and calamity the long-anticipated Age of Grace will begin, with the new humanity which will live serenely in the age of gold, in the reign of Saturn.

6

WHAT NOSTRADAMUS SAID

> *Was there, therefore, a god who wrote these things?*
> Goethe *Faust*, Act I.

No one can discuss prophecy without mentioning Nostradamus. The 966 quatrains of his famous *Centuries* contain many prophecies which go into great detail. But the quatrains are strewn about without any order in such a way that even if the beginning were found it would not be possible to continue them in the right order. They are usually vague, involved in the confused language of sybilline oracles, some literal and some symbolic. So much so that in the confusion between literal and symbolic one is left hardly understanding anything at all! If some are easy to understand, others are incomprehensible. He writes in the French of his day, mixed with Latin words with others made up by him and his own anagrams.

But why is the fame of Nostradamus as a prophet so great?

The truth is that Nostradamus has been understood only after the events he forecast have happened. He saw everything clearly in advance and even wrote the most outstanding names of people who took part in history before they were born but has given them in the form of an anagram to conceal them from readers. He writes Ripas instead of Paris, Chiren instead of Henric (Henry), Italy he calls Mesopotamia and says Sparta instead of a dictatorial regime, grasshoppers and locusts instead of aircraft, which, in his day, did not exist. He has written of the present day with the red sand the sign of the sickle as if it were contemporary history. He saw its momentary success and then its catastrophic fall, as with everything else that is based upon material things.

Nostradamus as Astrologer and Prophet (1503–66)

Michele Nostradamus was born at St. Rémy in Provence, France, on 14 December 1503 and knew well the Cabala, the Veda, the Gospels and above all, astrology. He possessed ancient books of his Hebrew ancestors who studied deeply the subjects that interested them and who devoted days and nights, staying up for hours with their astrolabes and other instruments, magic mirrors and divining rods, consulting writings in various languages as well as ancient parchments. He was an expert in Zodiacal things, and worked out the position of Jupiter, Mars and Venus and the other planets and their reciprocal aspects and was able to establish the facts and the times of the events in the lives of men in the centuries to come.

What Nostradamus wrote was an extraordinary mixture of scientific calculation and prophetic writings. Indeed, so exact were his prophecies and of such high standards, it is possible to establish certain details far more exactly as a result. He seems to limit his prophecies to the year 2,000, not calculated exactly, indeed, his prophecies could refer to another period of time in which roughly similar events took place. But he is really a prophet of the Age of Pisces, limiting his visions into that era. He knew quite well that after the evolution of humanity, men could be raised on to a higher plane, and thanks to the development of the powers of clairvoyance will be able to perceive a new light by means of their sharpened conscience. Their task is outlined by the sign the light gives them.

The obscurity of Nostradamus was deliberate and it enabled him to concentrate much more completely on the work he was doing. His method is rather like those who make riddles. It is, therefore, very difficult to unravel what he has carefully wrapped up in presentation and it is indeed impossible to give a date to any single event which he forecasts throughout his quatrains. Those which have been resolved have often helped to make the understanding of the passage more difficult instead of simpler! Some have taken them as works of fantasy, reading into them ideas which were not intended, while others have sought only to find a confirmation in them of their own imagination and their own preconceived ideas.

We will relate some of the quatrains whose prophecies have not yet come to pass, with the certainty that they will do so in future. But in what order they will take place we do not know. Nostradamus declared that he could put the date to all the quatrains. He has not done so. When he did it for the date of his own death, he blundered, yet described in accurate detail the way it happened. Dates belong to Man and only have a relative importance. It is the facts which matter.

The General Picture before the Details

We have anticipated the several commentators to the work of Nostradamus, but we note in particular the authors quoted in the bibliography. The events which should happen in the remainder of this century are reported in a sequence whose order is not guaranteed as the writing is like that of reconstructing a building without enough stones and ignoring the original plan.

The agreement of all the interpretations on the tribulations in the future is universal, but the dates vary in every instance. The pronouncements about a war in the second half of the century we are now in, rapid and destructive, as it will be waged with new types of weapons, also show a remarkable consistency.

According to P. Innocent Rissaut, the red revolutionaries would have the upper hand for eighteen months. Italy would be invaded from the north together with Sicily, Spain, Germany as far as the Rhine and then France. Paris would be burned down and destroyed for ever. The red forces will be formed, apart from the Russians, also by Germans, Turks and Arabs. Rome will be devastated. There would be a massacre of clergy. The Pope would be imprisoned and then die during the burning of the Vatican. A cardinal would also be killed. There would be a great schism with three popes at the same time: one Italian, one German and one Greek. They would all be killed in the course of a month.

The tremendous war would leave the north and the east (Palestine?) and would last two years. Missiles would be employed. There would be ten months of victory for the oriental invaders and then a new weapon would be brought into use, 'darts of the sky' Nostradamus calls them, and would devastate the principal cities of America, Britain, Russia and the Balkans. The war between East and West would come to an end after immense destruction.

From the confusion which would prevail in the two hostile camps a certain German emperor would profit and would take command of all the armies, the Asiatic and the European. He would put the 'German antipope' on the throne after the pope had fled who had been elected after the schism. He would be enthroned and proclaim the new 'Holy Roman Empire'. But this would only last seven months after which the Emperor and Antipope would be killed and their supporters slaughtered and hunted out.

Seven years later an Italian Grand Pilot and Grand Monarch, freed from the prison in which they had been placed by the German Emperor, would pacify the land and replace the legitimate pope on the throne. He would chase the 'pirates of the sea' and the hordes of barbarians out of Europe. He would give the Holy Places in Palestine to the church. This Grand Monarch, after ten years rule which was reasonably stable, would go to die in Palestine.

The Grand Monarch will be the founder of the Order of Cross Bearers who strive against the enemies of God, striking down anyone among them who could be the future Antichrist. He will be at the head of the ten kings. Then there will be one sheepfold and one pastor with a long period of peace.

According to this same P. Innocent Rissaut, Antichrist has already been born during the pontification of Pius XII in Palestine, at the time a comet appeared in the same year as the death of Pope Pacelli. But he will start his career towards 1980 and will be accepted as universal monarch about 2000 with the destruction of Rome. The final schism will take place then. The time of sadness will be shortened 'by the love of the elected'.

The evil exploits of Antichrist will last for three and a half years after which he will be killed. Humanity, after so much suffering, will be awaiting the new coming of Christ.

In the comments of other ancient manuscripts, variations of time and of order are found but the substance of the prophecy remains – a long war, persecutions, famine, with the addition of natural cataclysms which seem to accompany the confusion in men's minds after so many calamities.

Thus with wars and disasters we reach July 1999 which will witness the last invasion of the Asians and of Antichrist. But it will not come to an end with everything in ruins: it is only the surgical operation, sad but necessary, before the arrival of the New Humanity.

This is the tragic picture of the events, which, according to the comments of Nostradamus will take place in the period of time which precedes and follows the year 2000.

If all this can be condensed into such a short period of time the picture would be dark without parallel in history.

But, still outlining a general picture, we will give the reader the points we have discussed not only from Nostradamus but also from other accounts which have been cited and given in the bibliographies. They agree in tracing artificially a picture of future events according to several prophecies. The order of the events cannot be indicated clearly or in any definite way. But the substance of their message remains – with its exceptional gravity.

I. *The Protagonists*

The sickle, the Reds, the Arabs, of whom Nostradamus speaks frequently.

The Emperor of the North with his German antipope.

The Great Monarch and the Sacred Pontificate.

The Cross Bearers.

The ten Christian Kings of the world. Selim. The Romano-Belgian king.

The Ultimate Antichrist, Universal Monarch.

II. *The Dates and the Events*

Revolution in Italy and flight of the Pope.

Civil War in France and revolution in England. Revolts in America too.

Arab-Russian Invasion of Europe.

Temporary confirmation of red success, with violence, persecution and famine.

Renouncing of faith by catholic, antipope in Rome. Schisms. Holy Roman Empire proclaimed by the German Emperor and his puppet antipope.

War with China.

World uprising against communism with bloody results.

Natural disasters, earthquakes, epidemics, floods.

Pursuit of the invaders and re-establishment of the position of the Great Monarch and the Holy Pope.

Epoch of peace.

Return of war with alternating revolts and disasters.

Unpropitious action of the final Antichrist. Final war with the use of deadly weapons. Three days of darkness, signs in the sky. Ending of an epoch culminating with the Great Day. Total destruction of the impious. Satan cast into the abyss.

Coming of a Happy Age with a Humanity revivified and made spiritual.

I. The Protagonists

We will give a short description of the chief personalities of the age which we are examining.

(A) The German Emperor (of the North)

Among the events forecast for these years of confusion is also the proclamation of the Roman Emperor.

The holy Emperor will be proclaimed in Germany, says *Centuries* x, 31, the Israelites will find free places there; the Asiatic people want it as well as Carmania (France), but its supporters will be seen all over the Earth.

This will be verified when the Arabs open the gates for the invasion. This Emperor of the North, the great liar, as Nostradamus calls him, will be scouraged by Italy and particularly by the Church. It will never be satisfied with what it has, says *Centuries* IX, 45, Rome and France will never have had a worse tyrant.

The German Emperor will pretend to give himself up to the Pope, while pretending to help him, then giving himself away by his lies. The unwise action of this Emperor of whom we relate the actions when it concerns Rome and the pontificate will not last long : seven months of unlimited domination. Then he and the antipope whom he will raise, will be beaten and killed. (*Centuries* II, 55 and *Centuries* VI, 76). Thus the pseudo Roman Empire will fall, as it will rise, by violence.

(B) The Great Monarch

Dante in *De monarchia*, from the bards of his era, sees the 'Universal Monarchy' in advance, 'who so loves Man for his human consideration and asks him neither to perform tasks as a punishment nor what God thinks of him before calling him brother'. Eliminate in this way the diversions and the regions of contrast between men which have cost so much blood, and it will complete the unification in a converging point which is much higher.

The Great Monarch, according to the prophecy, will have to put everything in order before the last epoch. Of him St. Brigid writes that he will prohibit everyone from using arms, men will recognize God, Unity and Trinity, and there will be one flock and one Pastor.

Another forecast says:

The Grand Monarch (or Powerful King) will take God's side and annihilate the republics ... and will bring real peace on Earth.

According to *Centuries* I, 50, the Great King will be born in Italy and will be like a devastating tempest for the Orientals and their doctrine. When he appears all seven of them will vanish.

After seven years that the barbarian peoples of the north (the Russians) have taken the city of Jaffa, they will be dispersed by the Grand Monarch and by one of the princes of the celestial militia – St. Hildegarde, 1179.

He will destroy Turkey and discomfit the Emperor of the North, says another prophecy of a Cappucin monk of 1779.

Before Antichrist, there will arise in Italy a man so strong as to compare with Samson. He will be a native of Italy ... and will have descended from the noblest stock. This man, much loved by God, will free Lombardy from slavery and Italy from martyrdom. With permission from the Holy Father, besides, and of the Union (of the ten kings) he will enter Greece with his sailors and there lay waste many cities – Merlin 1640.

(C) *The Angelic Pastor*

There will be harmony and unity of action between the Grand Monarch and the Pope. In his prose prophecy Nostradamus says of him: 'He will have piety, virtue and the doctrine of returning the church to its original state. He will be called Angelico.'

The seven last popes will all be called angelic and the first of them will be Pius XII. He will be of the surviving monastic order of the Minor Friars because in the intervening time all the others will have been abolished as some outlived their usefulness and the others were dispersed during the terrible invasion. The pope who collaborates with the Grand Monarch will be the ideal pope, who has been looked for in vain for centuries, and who with his life and his work will be an example to all.

His actions will also put pressure on the unfaithful who will be converted.

Other prophecies declare: the new pope will be a great personality with deep holiness. With his example and spiritual charge and with the help of the Great Monarch who will fall in with his plans, he will do great things for religion.

The prosperity of the Lord will come down on to the distressed nations, a renowned guardian of souls will take his place on the papal throne with the protection of the angels ... Then a graceful king, a descendant of Pepin, will go on a pilgrimage to behold the splendour of the glorious papacy ... A similar prophecy declares: After having settled in the Roman City the King of Blois will place the regal tiara on the head of a great pope, the summit of the bitterness of the tribulation, which will force the clergy to live under the discipline of the apostolic age....

(D) *The Ten Kings*

Ten Christian kings will be allied to the Grand Monarch in the period between the wars, a happy if short period, when they will work for the re-establishment of peace. Nostradamus calls them 'kings' from the usage of his day, but they could merely be the governors of countries in a United Europe. [typed 30/12/72! J.G.G.] Among the ten, there is only one for Germany, who will be elected after the murder of the German Emperor (of the North) and the defeat of his followers.

In *Centuries* v, 74 it is said that: he will be born of Trojan (Italian) blood and German heart and will take on great powers; he will throw out the peoples of Arab stock, while bringing the Church back to its primitive greatness. He will, with the help of the Grand Monarch, eject all the Orientals to whom formerly the gate of the imperial tyranny was always open.

Another ally of the Grand Monarch was the person whom Nostradamus calls the Roman-Belgian king: He will be given the lance of a great King of the Orient. He will be supported by a warlike people of Belgian Gaul.

Olivario wrote in 1542: The Grand Monarch will have authority over his united kingdoms of Europe [written 1/1/73]. He will control the destinies of the world giving advice to every nation. He will be a king above all other kings. . . .

A prophecy attributed to Gioacchino (1200) declares that two kings, one in Greece and the other in Italy, will wage war against the Turks. These two kings will elect other eight kings and will be ten, and, all of them being Christians, will create the Roman Empire.

(E) *The Crucifers*

The Grand Monarch will be the founder of the order of the Cross (Crucifers). These men will form an army whose weapons will be arms, speeches and hospitality.

St. Francis of Paola wrote in 1507: God will raise up a very poor man with the blood of Constantine, who will bear the sign of the Cross on his breast ... such a man will be almost a saint in his boyhood and adolescence, then in his youth will be a great sinner, then will change his ways and become a saint. He will be frightened as was St. Paul. He will be the founder of the Crucifers. The Great Monarch and the Crucifers will dominate the world. He and his followers will reform the world. Those with him will be the holiest, best armed and the best-read men.

As for those with the cross on the breast their methods, above all, those of the initiates, will not seem very Christian. Indeed, according to S. Francesco de Paola, they will destroy the Mahometan sects entirely as well as the infidels: they will commit great massacres, and rivers and lakes will be seen formed of the blood of the infidels.

We are much taken aback at that idea of sanctity! The Cross on their banner is not enough, neither do we know if it is possible to reconcile their actions with the declaration that: they will carry the sign of God on their breasts and even more in their hearts. But, perhaps it will be the enthusiasm of beginners. This indeed seems confirmed by the expression: they will change . . . into the most faithful servants of God and will show that beforehand they were not Christians at all.

The army of the Crucifers will be called the Holy Union because, perhaps, it will be the armed forces of the Grand Monarch which will unite all the peoples of Europe at whose head will be the ten kings. The arms will be used to wound and kill. Their victory will, therefore, be physical, overpowering their opponents by physical force and not the conquest of their hearts, which is the only true way to win a victory.

II. *The Age of Calamities*

Reading the prophecies of Nostradamus is not, therefore, anything very comforting. It is indeed true that for two thousand years a pagan society, with the name Christian, has carried on the old way by killing, taking advantage over people and hurting them. Now that we are at the end of the cycle, it seems that this rhythm is becoming even more accentuated, because the prophecies foresee the unloosing of a wave of violence, and horror. Folly will seem to take hold of men while anarchy will upset men's minds and their society.

The blood of the great will be spilled . . . the nations will totter in great misery. Whosoever begs for alms will receive them. . . .

Naked and hungry, devoured by cold and by thirst, they will err in every way to the great scandal of everyone ... Women, the old and children will be menaced by death.

We have made nothing but war for centuries. Humanity must become satiated with it. But it goes on with invasions, sackings, massacres, ruination and disasters. As a result, they will get from this epidemics, scarcity, earthquakes and cataclysms. Nostradamus, and with him, almost all the seers and prophets, announces the New Age with the seventh millennium, but the last few kilometres of the journey is truly very disagreeable. P. Innocent Rissaut, in his commentary on *Centuries*, foresees a short peace between 1971 and 1980, and then, after 1980 the Third World War which will culminate in 1983 with a Russian victory, then peace for five years until in 1988 an alliance will be made or a successful American counter-offensive in 1989. The momentary triumph of the negative forces will upset the weak, whom they have not yet eradicated from inside their fortress, but who have not yet developed enough force to resist and then to win.

Michele de Socoa foresaw extraordinary events for 1983, 1988 and 1991. Two thousand years of history full of atrocities, according to many prophecies and comments of Nostradamus, will culminate in a world war. Similarly, Donato Piantanida says that there will be two world wars in the remainder of this century which afflicts humanity before the arrival of the Messiah. The use of atomic weapons seems to be foreseen by Nostradamus. The fearful sentence in *Centuries* II, 95 bears witness to this: The populated places will be rendered uninhabitable.

The commentators are almost in agreement that the time of calamities, which will last twenty-seven years, will have a brief period of peace for the martyrized people. Nostradamus speaks of numerous new arms, fire from heaven which strikes down people and things, darts from heaven, large lightly-armed horses on the battlefield. They use various names, made from the words in use in those days, to indicate, in sixteenth-century terms, bombs, guided missiles, bombers and other arms not yet invented. New stars will appear in the heavens making people think that the axis of the Earth has changed its position.

"The Bloody War will last 27 Years"

According to the various prophecies, partial war, but not yet atomic, and natural cataclysms will disrupt the life of men for many years, almost until the end of the century. When all this has come to an end hope will once again blossom forth in the minds of men. But it will be fighting alternating with hope in an ever-growing crescendo. Things that cannot be undone will occur towards the end of the century when Man, blinded with hate, spread by the final Antichrist, will have at his disposition murderous weapons of destruction that a science without morals has put at his disposal. Then the end of everything will be seen – total destruction. Life on this planet will seem extinct, completed by the enormous natural catastrophes which will finish the work. The apocalyptic vision will begin in 1966. From 1966 to 1972 war, struggles, persecutions and influence of the Sixth Antichrist. From 1979 to 1988 there will be another war and more ruin and the influence of the Seventh Antichrist. Those who had enough perception to foretell the dates declared that the years 1972–3 will be marked by the appearance of a Mahometan Antichrist who will prepare another invasion of Europe. Between 1973 and 1982 the invading armies will occupy Spain, Italy, Hungary and France until 1987. In 1987 the Pope will die a prisoner. In 1995 the final invasion of the Asiatics and Antichrist will take place.

The final conflict will take place between 1994 and 1996 when the Eighth and final Antichrist will appear and will end the history of the Christian world. The prophecies tell us that there will be twenty-seven years of wars and bloodshed. This is confirmed by *Centuries* VIII, 77 :

The third Antichrist will be almost annihilated, and his war will last twenty-seven years. The heretics will be killed, made prisoner and exiled. Blood from Antichrist's human body will redden the water.

Nostradamus forecasts that the present Adamic age will end around 2000. But long before these dates: the adversaries of Christ will begin to appear in ever increasing numbers, as St. Brigit has written. And today we are in the final epoch before the apocalypse. What Nostradamus means by the third Antichrist, whose war will last twenty-seven years is easy to understand. The graduation of Antichrist has taken place on a large scale. (1) the Roman Empire, (2) the French Revolution, and (3) Marxism. This time it is a collective and not a personal ideology.

A system like Marxism, set up with bloodshed, maintained by means of terror and in violation of the most elementary rights of Man, in which hatred is normal and has violence and the glorification of materialism as ends in themselves is the direct opposite of the dedicated life of Jesus Christ – love. Millions of people eliminated in fierce repressions, condemned to forced labour, unknown martyrs of a people repressed as if in an enormous prison are all tragic realities which have not served to open the eyes of the blind men in the West, still victims of a will o' the wisp.

An invasion of Arabs and Slavs?

Italy is so used to invasions which vary in type and having one master succeeding another that it has partly formed the character of the inhabitants. Nostradamus described other influences. In *Centuries* IV: 82 he says:

A mass of people draws near, coming from Slavonia (Jugoslavia), ancient Olestant will sack the city, much desolation will appear in Rumania, but it will not succeed in extinguishing the great flame.

From the Black Sea and from the Great Tartary, *Centuries* V, 34, tells us, one leader will go towards

France and another armed force coming from Armenia will occupy Constantinople. It will, therefore, be an invasion by Slavs. Or will the Russians not hesitate to make use of other nations? This seems confirmed in *Centuries* II, 29:

The Easterners will come from their homes to pass the Appennine Mountains and in Gaul the sky will be perforated (missiles?) and the water and the snow. Everyone will choke.

Again, in *Centuries* II, 39–40 it says: A little before the Italian-German conflict the French and the Spaniards will arm themselves strongly. The maternal home of the Republic will fall, and with a few exceptions all will be suffocated and die. Shortly afterwards, with little time between them, there will be a much greater tumult both by sea and by land and it will consist of both naval battles and land struggles.

According to Nostradamus the Arabs will take advantage of the disorder in Europe to rise in revolt. The Pope at the time of the Mahometan invasion of Italy could be he who is called by the motto *De mediaetate lunae* (from the middle moon). This comes in *Centuries* I, 9.

From the Orient he will see the Punic centre (Libya?) and will harass Adria (Italy) the descendants of Romulus. He will be accompanied by the Libyan fleet, threatening that of Malta and the islands nearby will be sacked.

The invader will come from the East (*Centuries* I, 9). He will disembark in various parts of the Adriatic coast. The small islands as well as Sicily and Sardinia will be ravaged.

Centuries V, 68: The Great Camel (the Arabs) will see and drink the waters of the Danube and the Rhine. They will not repent of it. Those of the Rhône will tremble with fear and even more so those of the Loire and the land near the Alps will be ruined by a plague of cockerels.

Nostradamus does not give any date for the Arab invasion, but gives the stages briefly. At first he announces that there will be an islamic incursion into southern Europe and in the Adriatic. While the West is divided (*Centuries* VII, 25) the ambition of Islam will grow. They will menace Spain (III, 20) and destroy Israel (VIII, 96). According to Ruir, who comments on Nostradamus in his book *The First and Last Events*, (ed. Medicis, 1953) the Mahometan horde under the order of the seventh Antichrist will land in 1973 on the coast of Europe, having converted and conquered the opposite shores. This will not be like the methods of the Western Nations in 1944 in a single spot, but will take place at a number of places at the same time in order to make disembarking easy. This will also be done by little fishing boats, which will leave Algeria under the command of Chinese captains, who will return quietly to their bases. The Chinese will have taken the place of the Russians.

Under the leadership of the 'Carthaginian' general, the negro-African advance will proceed by landing in Sicily and Sardinia (1974) and then in Rome (1976). Other landings will take place in several parts of Italy (1978) and then at Marseilles (1978) and that will be followed by the occupation of Paris (1981) and of the whole of France by Polish, Hungarian, Indian, Austrian and Italian reinforcements, who will have already become Mahometans!

France and Britain will suddenly realize the danger, and will advance to Genoa, centre of the fighting, but will have to retreat back to France rapidly because the Mahometans will advance once more to Provence and Marseilles. They will perform fearful atrocities. In Italy they will burn down churches and convents and finally the Vatican itself. Even an Antipope will associate with the Mahometans and will force the Christians to follow the cult of the Apocalyptic beast which will be established. In 1978 the conquest of Spain from the Mahometan Morocco will be achieved.

In 1987, according to this same Ruir, who has been

making such sad prognostications, the greatest penetration of Marxist materialism from Asia will take place. So much so that nine-tenths of the world will fall under its dominion, including Australia and Canada. In this same year, according to him, the Pope *de Mediaeta Lunae*, after fifteen years of rule, will be made prisoner by the Mahometans and be guillotined by the Black Sea. Other prophecies say that the Pope will die as a result of a shipwreck. The temporary supremacy of the Arabs, Chinese and Russians has made several prophets foretell their victory over Israel, and the ending of Great Britain as a world power.

The great collapse of the British people (before 1980?) will soon begin in the Tuscan Sea (or in the Gulf of Genoa), declares the seer. And that will happen because 'they got under way far too late' and because of their occult methods.

The Shortcomings of France

Among the causes of the collapse of Europe Nostradamus cites particularly the negligence and discord in France. Everyone knows its opposition for many years to European unity, opposition stemming from shortsighted nationalism, which led the way to the Russo–Mahometan invasion. The foolish spirit of *grandeur* will end in a bad dream – in desolation. So *Centuries* I, 18 tells us:

Owing to the negligence and discord in France the way will be open for the invasion of Mahomet. The land and sea of the Seine will be impregnated with blood and the port of Marseilles will be covered with the wrecks of steamships and sailing ships.

The invasions will come from the sea (I, 29) and from the land (IV, 37). And France will have a huge bloodbath.

For Those who Tried to Save Themselves by Money!

Things will go badly for those who thought of putting their money in Swiss banks. Indeed *Centuries* IX, 44 warns:

Emigrate, oh emigrate, from Geneva as many of you as possible as the gold of Saturn will change into iron. The Anti-Czar will exterminate everyone. But before this event a sign will be seen in the heavens.

Not only, therefore, invasions, but sackings and slaughter. This is told us in *Centuries* IX, 12:

The richly-decorated images in silver of Diana and Mercury will be found in the lake. The seller of statuettes, looking for more clay to fashion, will be covered in gold, both he and his wares.

The Rev. Innocent Rissaut declares that the richly-decorated statues of Diana are money and titles belonging to the Church and those of Mercury the result of business done by the Vatican. If Nostradamus said that! . . . It will all be found in the lake. The seller of statuettes could be those mind-benders who wished to look for new clay to change the laws of God and will be covered with gold by the antipope and his followers.

The Defeat of the Invaders

After years of calamities and struggles there will eventually be liberation.

The Barbarians will be put to flight as far as Tunis. On the sea the Red Captain will be captured together with his pirates. The false successor to the Pope will wander in desert and wild places. The Reds will be cast into the abyss of a deep gorge.

The invaders will be defeated in a great battle near the Alpine passes by the work of 'Gallo'. According to *Centuries* V, 13, he will be a Romano–Belgian king, whom the prophecy does not define any better than the man who will pursue the men from Libya.

The Romano–Belgian king will annihilate the barbarian

forces with great savagery and with just as much fury will chase the men from Libya from Hungary to Greece.

The allied powers of the Third World War will not be the same as those of the previous one (France, Russia, Great Britain, U.S.A.). According to *Centuries* II, 38, one of them (Russia?) will be so burdened that when war breaks out again they will no longer be allies.

It will be a war of recovery. XI, 94 says that 'the . . . enemies of the sickle' will unite, the strongest nation (U.S.A.) will pass to the defence, but its weaker allies will be assaulted. Prussia (that is Germany) and Turkey will be on the side of the barbarians. In *Centuries* IX, 51 is written:

Against the seven red powers they are arrayed as one, by fire, water, steel, rope they will be consumed. At the point of death those who intrigued, with one exception, will be ruined.

The elements of nature will be against the Reds. Those who weaved plots died. One of them was saved, but he bore many wounds. That fellow, elsewhere, is called 'the partisan of the seven'. The interpreter of Nostradamus, E. Ruir, quoted already, says that America will intervene, landing an army in Portugal, freeing the Mediterranean countries and make prisoner the Mahometan Antichrist who will be brought to justice at Constantinople.

A Pause in the Torment

This will be, unfortunately, only a short space of serenity between so much fighting.

After a great human struggle, says *Centuries* II, 46, another, larger one will break out. There will be rain, blood, fighting, hunger, fire and plague, in the sky 'fire on a large spark' will be seen.

The last phase and the renovation of time will continue to draw near. Therefore the outbreak of this major struggle fits the pattern. At the same time an enormous use of missiles is forecast. Now there will be a rain of fire, blood of children and all the consequences of a war which perhaps will flare up unexpectedly. Then there will be a total renewal at the beginning of the century.

Italy pacified

In *Centuries* IV, 77, it is declared that Selim, the Christian king of the world, after having driven the pirates from the sea, pacified Italy, and reunited the kingdoms, died, wishing to be buried in holy ground. Round this figure whom Nostradamus calls Selim wonderful fantasies by innumerable commentators have been woven. Perhaps it is an anagram, indicating the place where he came from, or something else, now forgotten. As with other names one only knows the true identity afterwards. But it is he, the victorious leader, who will bring back peace after so many tribulations. The victory of the 'Great Selim' over the Turkish Empire is indicated likewise in VI, 76, where he is called 'The Eagle' who will be acclaimed. It treats of a Roman returned to life. That of Selim will be an ideal government – human rule guided by angels as X, 42 declares, adding that it will last 'for a long time'. For how long? It does not say. It will be a truce, as VIII, 95 declares:

The Seductor will be thrown in the ditch and chained up until a certain time. The clergy united, the chief among his flock, greeting them who will be all so contented.

There will be a harmony of government between Selim the Monarch and the Pope. In these times many will turn to the faith. Piantanida thinks that the Pope who is mentioned here is the one who is meant by the motto *De labore solis* (by the work of the sun), one of the seven ideal popes, the last but one of which will 'prove supreme'.

With the disappearance of the Grand Monarch the beginning of chaos will start. And this second period will be more tragic than the first. The final inexorable collision approaches. Satan is born in the worst of men, Antichrist, to impersonate all the forces of evil which will take part in the ultimate assault. But it will prove the worst defeat. Time will move quickly and events will follow one another very fast.

Sooner or later, says I: 56 – a great change will be made, extreme horrors and vendettas if the moon (the Church) were not guided by its Angels; the sky will turn at an angle.

The fury of negative anger is against religious expression and in this way: The Church will be persecuted by God and the sacred temples will be spoiled: the son will put a shirt on to his naked mother when the Arabs will be allied to the Poles.

Because of this we will be able to undergo a complete change which will be a tremendous test for humanity.

III. *The Final Antichrist*

In *Centuries* IX, 10, Nostradamus said that he would be born with a monk and a nun as parents, that they would abandon him and that he would be brought up by a pig-rearer. Is that a symbol? Or is it the literal truth? However, he will be someone who has escaped from the extermination of the war which will have just finished. With his astuteness and his hypocrisy he will succeed in taking everyone in, even the Grand Monarch. Indeed will it be he who succeeds the Grand Monarch and who until that moment will appear very different? It seems like it from VI, 57 which says:

He who holds high office in the kingdom shall have a red cap in the hierarchy, will reveal himself rough and cruel and will make many people fear when he succeeds the Grand Monarch.

Before he reveals himself he will live in a concealed manner until his hour comes. Nostradamus reveals even the date of his appearance together with the exploits of this horrible person.

The year will be 1999 and in the seventh month when a great king of horror will be seen in the sky to revive the great king of the Huns – before and after his coming Mars will reign happily. (*Centuries* X, 72).

This new Attila, the great king of Horror will come down with his aerial forces and spread death and destruction everywhere. Then Mars (war) will be in absolute control with all the sad consequences. We shall be at the culmination of the rigorous test of humanity. Antichrist, the second beast of the Apocalypse, will find his most propitious moment for his destructive action.

This terrible coming of the 'King of Horror' which we are told with certainty will be in October 1999 (the seventh astrological month) leaves us puzzled. It has been proved that events do not occur according to the dates foretold for them. At the dawn of 2 July 1566 when Nostradamus died and his inanimate corpse was found, it was remembered that he had foretold instead the date of November 1567 for the end of his prognostications. He had erred by more than a year. Another unfortunate prophecy about a date made by the same Nostradamus was forecasting that the election of Pope Paul V would take place in 1600, but which really took place in 1605 (cf. X 91). The prophet foresaw the event but not the date. It is therefore quite logical to deduce that we do not need to take any notice of the dates of the prophecies. The events which are to come are described with exactitude, but do not take place exactly when they have been foretold.

Here is the great enemy of the human race – as Nostradamus tells us in X, 10 – who will be worse than his grandfather, father and son, sowing works of death on a grand scale with steel, fire and water in a sanguinary and inhuman way.

His actions will lead to universal war and the ruin of the papacy. This is what 1, 4 has to say:

In the universe a king will arise who will not reign or live very long, when he loses the fishing boat (the papacy), will come into even greater trouble.

The only comfort in all this gloom is that the troubles will not last very long. Indeed it is written in the Gospel that the time will be shortened to favour the Elect. But having touched the bottom, events will begin to improve. The Seer of Salon tells us that the last Antichrist will not be collective but a single person, in this way agreeing with the Apocalypse.

At the time of the Great War which will destroy Paris and lay the Vatican waste, at the same moment when the Pope and the great French king will unite their forces to assure victory for the Christian west, Antichrist will be born of a monk and a nun. The little boy will be born with two teeth in his mouth when a rain of stone will descend on Paris. . . .

A few years later there will be not enough corn and barley to feed those who are famished with hunger....

He to whom they will give the paternal light impregnated with the spirit of darkness will be born in the abyss and the city of infinite (damage).

The Abomination of Desolation is fixed for the end of the sixth millennium which is at the end of the present century. After many calamities, bloodshed, wars and cataclysms one can easily believe that the sole desire of men will at last be for peace and love. Unfortunately the prophecies seem to foretell only the bad. *Centuries* 1, 16 says:

When the symbol of the sickle (Marxism) has flooded the Earth like the water from a pond it will have reached the greatest extent of its expansion; the world will be in a state of general misery, humanity struck down by epidemics, cursed by war and murder. The century will be drawing to its close.

However, the terrifying arsenal of atomic bombs and new arms will remain for the final act.

It is obvious that the great deception of those who adore the Beast seek benefit for themselves but in actual fact find only fighting and misery. Many of them are completely lost and they have no hope at all, deprived of their faith. And the Abomination of Desolation of Holy Scripture gives humanity a destiny no better than that of animals.

In the mysterious plan which foreordains life, Marxism, for men who are not developed spiritually, is an instrument of deception and ruin. It is presented as the redeemer and saviour of mankind and understands the works of the false prophets. Instead of raising the humble it raises the followers themselves in the social scale, gives them authority, fine clothes and sumptuous dwellings in which to live. Having become powerful themselves, they ally themselves with other powerful people, renouncing love. In this way they betray their mission and are rejected.

The Final Defeat of the Sons of Darkness

When the Antichrist, perhaps installed in Rome itself, which will then have become the 'home of the Malignant', thinks that he has confirmed his power for ever, his end will come.

Centuries IX, 83 tells us: when the sun reaches 20° in Taurus (11 May) the Earth will shake so much that the grand theatre (where Antichrist will be found surrounded by his followers) will collapse, burying everyone. The sky and the ground will be darkened. Then God and His forces will overcome the infidel.

In a united demonstration of power, which the Evil leader wished to be deified, all was suddenly changed to disaster. This seems to be foretold in II, 92:

Fire will be seen on Earth and the colour of gold in the sky. Struck from on high he has not been able to realise the wonderful event (perhaps a bogus ascension). There will be great human slaughter, the important prince will be captured . . . the onlookers will die and the proud will be put to flight.

The reign of the liar, elected universal monarch four years before (in December) will finish in a depressing enough way on 11 May. His followers will be persecuted without pause until they are wiped out. Natural events and cataclysms will finish the work.

The Sons of Darkness, guided by Satan, born in Antichrist, having sown their seed of hatred and blood-shed will be defeated by the Sons of Light, led to final victory by the Word itself.

A lot of people do not quite understand that some things will have to take place before these happy events. They will not happen in a short time. They will be a long series of events which will follow one another in the course of many years with truces and fighting coming alternately. Years of worry and trouble which seem the longer by the burdens of the times, by the pains which make the time seem to drag longer. This is a purification and a preparation which is necessary and which will have its end in the Great Day in which, as in a finale, everything will be completed with the rapidity of light.

And then the dawn of the New Age will break.

The End of an Epoch

Nostradamus says that this will occur around 2000. *Centuries* I, 48 says this about it:

The reign of the Moon (the Church) will run for twenty years, the monarchy will last for seven thousand more years, when the sun will take up the days which it has lost, then my prophecy will be understood and completed. But let us return to the argument in x, 74: At the fulfilment of the great seventh number, there will appear wraiths from the Hecatombs, not far from the great age of the Millennium, when the dead will rise from their tombs. But this seems like the announce-ment of the second resurrection after a thousand happy years.

After twenty centuries of rule by the Church, at the seventh millennium, the prophecy will be completed. The dead will rise for the Second Coming of Jesus. During the long years of struggle and disaster everyone will be given the chance to know what is going on and to choose. The bad is only a façade, it has no consistency in it like the shade compared with the sun. Pain has this function of illumination and purification. God wishes all men to be saved as St. Paul has written (I Timothy 2 : 4).

Infinite Love works by looking for the good be it pure or sometimes through long works and unheard-of sufferings.

In the symbolism of Nostradamus the moon represents the Church, the moon, which reflects light. With the setting of the moon the sun itself rises, Christ. From *Centuries* x, 73:

The Great Judge will judge time present and time past. The future world (that is to say, those who have not listened) will be recognized as disloyal by the judging clergy, which will be repudiated as they themselves wearied Christ.

Other men will form the New Humanity. They will be new men who will have another conception of life who, as *Centuries* II, 13 tells us, will consider the true date of birth the day that they die; the spiritual body which, after the coming of Christ, will take on something more than the animal, will never again be sacrificed to existing without the spirit and which will never again know death.

7

THE DAWN OF THE THIRD ERA

Singular prophecies are contained in a book, *The Dawn of the Third Era*, by Karmohaksis, published in Rome in 1959, which we are about to relate. The expression 'Third Era' is used exactly in the same sense as it is by Gioacchino da Fiore. The years until 2033 will be characterized by great signs of renovation. Nature will take part in creating new surroundings for the New Humanity. Therefore the old humanity will disappear and the New Humanity will take its place. A large proportion of present-day humanity will disappear to give way to the new men.

These are the general outlines. But at the head of these predictions are even included the dates on which the events will take place. This is a highly imprudent thing to do in prophecy. This is almost always a disappointment when the time comes for fulfilment, because the coming to pass of great cosmic events is not bound to the human calendar. Events succeed one another when they are ready to do so, and by the law of cause and effect can occur later, sooner or in another way than expected – it is a series of happenings and not a series of dates.

The year 1970 is considered in these prophecies as the beginning of the real end of the present age. For fifteen years there will be cataclysms of all types, earthquakes, tidal waves, volcano eruptions, cyclones, and water-spouts at sea and in marshland. Huge areas of land will be submerged by water in the whole planet.

But the vision of the 'prophet' wishing to be too precise in his dating of events results in not getting his time-scale correct. In other words, he makes a mistake. For instance the tidal wave forecast for 1970 which would submerge Ostia did not take place. But the disorders in Paris, which we were told would take place with bloodshed took place before the date they were expected. But for Paris the prognostication was even more gloomy because for that year in addition was forecast the destruction of the city by fire from above. Things that were forecast in other prophecies that were going to take place did not do so in that year. Of greater importance is the fact that the Russian invasion, and the fall of Queen Elizabeth II, forecast for a long time in many prophecies, did not take place in the year forecast for them by Karmohaksis, that is, in 1970. This shows how hazardous it is to place a date against any prophecy either if the event takes place on its own or is in a series of events. We will now quote the prophecy verbatim.

1972. The city of Rome will be partly destroyed, including St. Peter's, Castel San Angelo and the lower parts of the city which will remain submerged.

In a period of about three years and in two or three stages as a result of tidal waves and the lowering of the ground, other parts of the Eternal City, and to be exact, in Rome the water will reach as high as the second step from the top of the flight up to the church of Santa Maria Maggiore – or from the church of San Giovanni.

After St. Peter's has been submerged, the Pope will transfer his seat to San Giovanni.

As a result of these planetary disasters, especially earthquakes and tidal waves which will follow one after another, a great part of the peninsula between 1972 and 1975 will be covered by the sea – and worst affected will be southern Italy as a result of the movement of the land. The peninsula as such will as a result, be divided into three sections. Sicily will disappear and also will Sardinia, Naples will be destroyed; part of the Po plain and part of Tuscany will be submerged; Milan will be badly damaged.

All the countries of Europe, to a greater or lesser degree will share the lot of Italy. Most badly affected will be Belgium, Holland, Russia, Germany, France, Spain and Portugal. Great Britain will escape almost entirely.

Other grave disasters all over the world are confirmed (Asia, Africa, North and South America and Australia). The Sahara will be submerged.

In all the countries of Europe and also in the countries of the other continents the organization of the state, the civil and social authorities will as a result be completely destroyed and the people will be without a guide. Man, in most cases, will return to the state of a caveman, forced to eat grass for food.

The magnitude of the disaster and thus the importance of the human losses in the various countries will be reflected in the behaviour that Earthly creatures will have shown until the day of the 'end of time'. At the moment when these prophecies will come to pass the percentage of men which can be saved are as follows: At Rome, 25 per cent. In all Italy, 20 per cent. In the rest of Europe, 18 per cent. In the whole world 53.5 per cent.

At the same time as the submersion and destruction just mentioned, this period of maximum activity will witness, as has already been pointed out, between 1970 and 1985, the creation of new lands. A continent of huge dimensions (about the size of Australia) will emerge between Australia and New Zealand and in the Atlantic part of the continent of Atlantis will be seen again.

The area of the part of Atlantis which will appear will be more or less a quarter of the other new continent in size, but will reveal fabulous riches in its bounds. The ruins of the capital of Atlantis, Cernés [Jacqueline Murray, the expert on Atlantis, called the capital Chalidocean in her books. J.G.G.] the city of the golden gates, will emerge once more and among these ruins will be the remains of the great temple of Poseidon with its crystal cupola almost intact. The cupola will no longer be supported on its seven brass columns, as they will have collapsed. Objects will be found made of a metal completely transparent unknown to us and other precious remains of the flourishing civilization of the red races, whose land disappeared as a result of the abuse made of the power given from on high to those people.

All these remains together with the cataclysms which will strike our planet will constitute a stern warning to all people and which will call them to a way of life which is always right and will not offend the Powers on High.

Between 1970 and 1975 ships of a new type will be built, completely spherical with jet propulsion with the advantages of a greater velocity than at present and a much greater stability.

1985. Men will begin to love one another like brothers and the light of the spirit will begin to shine and work with greater intensity all the time. Probably world government will be instituted by 1985.

The crust of the Earth will have undergone a gradual displacement in respect of its axis of rotation and the North Pole will be to the north-east of where it now is from the direction of Great Britain and in actual fact on a parallel of longitude which passes through Scandinavia. The movement of the Earth's crust will have begun before the prophecies in this section of the book have come to pass.

Climatic condition will change. Italy is destined to become an arid and cold country while in certain zones of Russia there will be the same mild and temperate climate that exists in the Italian peninsula today.

After 1985 the cataclysms will begin to lessen gradually and then with increasing speed until they come to an end in 2006.

1995. This year the foreign Pope will die and the Church will remain without a leader for three years and on three occasions attempts will be made to choose an Italian Pope.

In 1995 an epidemic of a completely incurable illness

will make its appearance but it will be over by 1997.

At the beginning of 1995 it will be possible to start rebuilding in easy stages the governments of the state and local authorities which have been destroyed, and by 1998 there will be quite noticeable results. The work or reconstruction will proceed fast, with enthusiasm and wideness of vision. Atomic bombs and missiles will no longer be made. Armies will be run down gradually. In the reconstruction of the large centres of population it will become the custom that the long distance and through traffic will run on top of the houses.

2000. The light of the Third Age, the age of the Holy Spirit, will begin to shine out brightly among the people; a new sense of mental peace will make up the innermost feelings of Man, and faith in God will become ever-increasingly alive, deeper and have more feeling. The Church, in which the various schisms will be healed will be reconstructed. Well-being and prosperity will go on growing at an ever increasing rate. The six great nations will reach their full development and nearly all the beings on Earth will rejoice in the possession of medium-istic powers.

For 2033 Karmohaksis forcasts the coming of a Pope, who has received a vision from a high Heavenly being, who will be 'the first to assert the principles of the Third Age.'

However, the 'principles' have already been pro-claimed for some time. But they have not yet been put into practice.

8

PROPHECIES ABOUT ROME AND THE LAST POPES

In prophecy the fate of the city of Rome is usually bound up with that of the Papacy. This is quite understandable as for many centuries the Popes' temporal power identified one with the other.

I. *Prophecies about Rome*

In May 1954 the rumour of the immediate end of the world spread around Rome. It was talked about with apprehension in offices, in the streets and in the churches. Scepticism and indifference have not completely deadened the minds of men. The most informed even knew the exact date: Monday, 24 May 1954. It was said that the Pope had had a vision. This was denied by the Vatican authorities who said it was a complete lie and added that there was nothing in the rumour. In the papers at that time appeared news of this strange phenomenon of popular feeling.

What was its origin? A few days earlier the rising of part of the floor of the Colosseum had been noticed, where it borders on the Via Labicana. On the thousand-year-old walls of the amphitheatre conspicuous cracks were noticed. The scaffolding put up for the repair had caught public fantasy. The Romans in the older parts had evidently not forgotten the verses of Giggi Zanazzo:

> *When the Colosseum crumbles away*
> *All the world will fade away.*

There was also the prophecy of the British monk, the Venerable Bede (673–735) which linked the fall of the Colosseum with that of Rome and the whole world. This is what he said:

Coliseus stabit et Roma; quando cadet Coliseus, cadet

et Roma, quando cadet Roma, cadet et mundus. (As long as the Colosseum stands Rome will stand, when the Colosseum falls Rome will fall too; when Rome falls, the rest of the world will come to an end too).

This is a prophecy which has been in existence for a very long time. Tertullian (Apocalypse, 32), confirms that when Rome, according to the Sybilline books, is reduced to a pile of rubble, there will be no doubt at all that the end of everything as we know it is at hand.

Rome will Disappear only at the End of the World

In contrast with other cities which will disappear during the wars and the cataclysms which will take place beforehand, the desolation of Rome will take place at the end of time when the Antichrist will appear.

P. Innocent Rissaut is convinced that the Antichrist will not be able to appear until Rome is destroyed and the Papacy suppressed with the murder of Peter the Roman. There will be much woe, ruin and damage, but the final end of Rome will not take place before the end of the Earth. It will not occur before. The name of Eternal City means what it says, although given without prophetic insight, and refers to the place which will last while all the Earth lasts. Can the Romans, therefore, remain calm while these things go on? Not likely, if they believe all the calamities which so many prophecies have foretold as referring to Rome.

Saint Ambrose declared that the second coming of Christ would most certainly be preceded by two inescapable facts: firstly the destruction of Rome; and secondly the appearance of Antichrist on Earth. Lattanzio in his day was persuaded that the end of the world would take place, but was perplexed because Rome was great and flourishing. From that he deduced that the end lay a long way ahead in the future.

Rome, considered as *caput mundi* (head of the world) had of course to be maintained as the centre and source of stability of the world, and its future and its fate were bound up with the common destiny of the civilized peoples as were then known. On account of its important position, exposed to every wind that blows, it has been the target for political invective, such as the famous one by Dante and religious attacks by other Christian faiths, and most frequent of all have been the arrows aimed at it by prophets. It has indeed been identified with Babylon, the home of Antichrist. But in all this invective, even more so than with truth, it is clear that the language is influenced by partisanship and with anger which harms the city not at all!

It was a heavy task to unite peoples who were different and divided against one another, to give laws to all men. The rule of the emperors was therefore a mixture of steel and clay. As a result the end of Rome is considered in world history as the end of an epoch of great importance.

The Changes which Threw it into Confusion

Michele Nostradamus refers to Rome in several volumes of *Centuries*, his well-known prophecies. To make an analysis of them would need a book in itself because he speaks of Rome both when he refers to the changes in the history of Italy, and also when he writes of the Pope. For our studies, we shall choose only those which are connected with the periods of history which we are discussing and those which have a bearing on the end of the world.

The venerable Batolomeo di Saluzzo, who died in 1605, fixed as the beginning of the 'grand plan' for the city of Rome, the days which will follow a 14 June, without being definite about the year.

The Turkish Moor will be seen roaring like a bull
Doing great damage with iron and fire.

Those who collect dates and names in order to draw conclusions, will realize that we do not know how much truth there is in this.

One of the commentators on Nostradamus, Barbault, foresaw the landing at Anzio of the Arabs in 1976 who will destroy Rome. Antichrist was seen among the Arabs. But we think that many interpretations are, at least, too hasty. In whatever manner, Rome will certainly not be spared from invasion.

Rome will be covered increasingly with ruins: Suor Imelda, 1872.

Nostradamus declares: In the city of Rome where the German (the Emperor of the North) will have entered almost at the same time as the Asiatic and Mahometan enemy. From the Italian countryside round Rome to the sea a terrible church (ideologically) will have the seduction of a siren. The Church of God will be persecuted and religious buildings confiscated. The ruins which will be made as a result will make all the Romans quake with fear, their great city will be a prey to corruption, a republic will plunder its monarchy and desecrate its churches.... The revolutionary spirit, scarcely struck down at its birth, will be born again in Italy with two heads.

De Fontebrune interprets the meaning of the two heads as a red chieftain who will govern Italy in disorder and a false pope.

Paolo Orisio, in Book II, chapter 4, explaining 'Septem capita septem montes' (seven heads and seven mountains) of the Apocalypse, says that Rome towards the end of time will stray away from the Christian faith and from Roman Catholicism to turn to ancient sins and after having driven out the Pope and killed the priests and church dignitaries will achieve a power greater than in ancient days. It will persecute the church with many deaths. But when it feels eternal and happy, it will witness its own downfall at the hands of the ten kings.

There will be great troubles for Rome at the hand of the Emperor of the North during the seven months in which this tyranny with its Antipope will rage.

The great city of the Volsci, says Nostradamus in *Centuries* VI, 98 will be ruined, defiled, and pestilence will be rife. It will be pillaged and its temples violated. The two rivers (Tiber and Anio?) will be reddened with blood.

Centuries II, 93 also announces the destruction of the Castel Sant'Angelo and of the Vatican. Rome will be devastated and sacked, the Pope made prisoner and replaced by an Antipope chosen by the Emperor of the North. (German.)

But in the times of greater affliction behold a mysterious figure will arise once more, an ancient shadow which has not been placated, an enemy of Rome. Nostradamus sees it advancing threateningly. In *Centuries* I, 9 the word Punic is mentioned. They will be seen to harass the descendants of Romulus. As already pointed out, E. Ruir deduces that the 'Carthaginian' leader, in command of the invasion accompanied by the Libyan fleet, will devastate Rome in 1976. Will it perhaps be a Karma which will be fulfilled? It seems that Nostradamus confirms this in *Centuries* II, 30:

> *One of the infernal allies of Hannibal*
> *Who is reborn, terror of mankind*
> *And even more horrible than the worst news*
> *Will be seen by the Romans, alluring them*
>   *from Babylon.*

But the ultimate ruin of Rome will be the work of Antichrist. Nostradamus calls Rome the daughter of Aurora, in other editions 'of Amore' – love making an anagram of Roma, the Italian form of her name, as if she had Amor, love, and calls her 'refuge of Malsano' because probably Antichrist will not be able to hold her as his temporary headquarters. The Seer says: she will be a slave more than four times and when she sees a prodigy, her time of trial shall be near. (*Centuries* VI, 100.)

But Rome will not be destroyed by Man. Nature will rise up with the force of its elements. Towards the end of time an immense cataclysm will make the waters of the sea rise up and submerge all the lower part of the peninsula from Sicily to lapping against the Roman theatre at Fiesole.

A flood so great and sudden that there will be no one to attack it nor the place to do so, writes the Seer in *Centuries* VIII, 16. Thus the ancient spot which was the 'rose of the world' will be submerged under the waves.

II. *The Prophecies on the Papacy*

The prophecies about the Papacy forecast very dark days for the Church. They are saints, seers, astrologers, divines, soothsayers which have given this very gloomy picture of times to come. Here are some of their sayings:

A fugitive Pope, followed by four cardinals only, will take refuge in Cologne. (Helena Walraff, 1790.)

The Church is stained purple with blood like the angel. It will be bathed in blood. (Katharine Emmerich, 1822.)

Russia will march on all the nations of Europe, especially on Italy and will raise its banner on the Cupola of St. Peter's. (Sister Elena Aiello, 1959.)

The Vision of Pius X

During a solemn audience for the General Chapter of the Franciscans, in 1909, those present, greatly wondering, saw the head of the Pope nod forward on to his breast. His eyelids closed and Pius X fell into a deep sleep which lasted a few minutes, during which time no one dared make the slightest movement. A little time later, the Pope opened his eyes and those with him saw agitation and horror in them. Pius X rose up from his seat and cried in an anguished voice: 'What I have seen was terrible. Will it be me or my successor? I do not know. What is certain is that I have seen the Pope fleeing from the Vatican, the priests carrying his body. Do not tell anyone this while I am alive.'

Those present were astounded by the force with which the Pope had said these words. Before he died, he is supposed to have said: 'I see the Russians at Genoa.'

Given the reserve in all the manifestations of his personality, and that there is no official record of this, we have to rely on books written by witnesses which refer to this astonishing incident.

From the time of Pius x, no Pontiff has left Rome or the Vatican in such a tragic way.

Will it come to pass in the future? The fact is that it does agree with many other prophecies.

The Prophecies of Don Bosco

In the life of S. John Bosco, many facts are told which show that he, in no small way, was endowed with exceptional qualities, a sixth sense developed so much that he could visualize and foresee things which other people ignored. But knowing well how easy it is to make mistakes in this field he used to say in argument 'Do not call me a prophet until the things I have said have come to pass.'

The prophecy written on stone which with one sentence describes a most tragic situation is ascribed to Don Bosco:

The horses of the Cossacks will drink at the fountain of St. Peter's.

What we are going to relate are the prophecies contained in the very rare first edition (see G. B. Lemoine, *Biographical Memories of Don Bosco*) about the stormy times which will sweep across the world, Italy and the Papacy in the next few years.

First Prophecy of Don Bosco

(Extract from Volume IX, pages 79–84). It was written and sent to Pope Pius IX in 1870. The night before the Epiphany 1870, Don Bosco had a vision in a dream and we retell below the part of this that referred to Rome and to Italy:

And you, Italy, land of benediction, have you been immersed in desolation? ... Not your enemies but your friends. Do not hate your sons who ask for the bread of faith and who, not finding that, break it up. What will you do? Batter the pastors, disperse the flock so that he who sits in the seat of Moses will look for good pastures and the flock will follow in a docile manner and feed. But above the flock and above the pastors my hand presses; famine, pestilence and war will break out so that the mothers will weep for the blood of the sons and husbands who die in enemy territory.

And what will happen to you, Rome, ungrateful, effeminate but superb city? You will be brought to such a state that still people will look for no better city, will admire your Sovereign (Pope), if not your luxury, completely forgetting that you are on the point of being brought down, your Golgotha. Now you are old, falling, unarmed deprived; yet with your enslaving word making the world tremble.

Rome! I will come to thee four times!

In the first coming I will strike your land and its inhabitants. In the second I will bring massacre and ravage the country to your walls. Will you then not open your eyes? I will come the third time, and beat down the defence and the defenders and at the command of the Father, I will inaugurate the reign of terror with fear and desolation.

But my people will know how to flee away, my law is always broken, therefore I will come a fourth time. Woe to you if my laws are still a vain name for you! Prevarication will succeed in both the learned and the ignorant. Your blood and the blood of your sons will wash the confusion which you have made of the laws of your God.

Wars, pestilence and hunger are the whips with which I will strike the pride and the malice of men. Where, oh rich, are your riches, your splendour, your villas and your mansions? They have become the refuse in the squares and the streets!

But you, oh priests, why have you not hastened to weep between the vestibule and the altar, invoking the ending of the chastisement? Why do you not take the shield of faith and go on to the roof-tops into the houses, on the streets, in the squares and into every place, even those difficult to reach and take there the message of my words? Do you ignore that it is the terrible sword with two cutting edges that overthrows my enemy and breaks the anger of God and man? These things will come inexorably one after the other. Events will take place too slowly.

But the august Queen of the Sky is present. The power of the Lord is in her hands; her enemies will be dispersed like mist.

The venerated Old Man will be reclothed in all his former garments. Then a violent hurricane will break out. Iniquity is finished and sin has come to an end and before two full moons of the month of flowers have passed the Iris of peace will blossom on Earth.

The great Minister will see the Wife of his King clothed in fine garments. All over the world a sun so bright will be seen, which has not been witnessed from the flame of Cenaculus until today, and which will not be seen until the final end of time.

The Second Prophecy of Don Bosco (24 May–24 June 1874)

This prophecy seems to be particularly concerned with our times (the dark night) and the future.

There was a dark night, men were no longer able to make out which was the road to take to return to their past, when there appeared in the sky a most magnificent light which revealed the road to the travellers as if it were midday. In that moment a multitude of people were seen, women, men, girls, monks, nuns and priests with the Pope at the head, coming out of the Vatican and taking up the form of a procession.

But behold, a furious storm broke out, which obscured the light somewhat, and a battle seemed to break out between the light and dark. Meanwhile the procession reached a small square covered with dead and wounded, who appeared to be crying for help in a loud voice.

The lines of the procession began to break up. After walking for a space of time which corresponds to two hundred sunrises, everyone realised that they were no longer in Rome. Alarm spread through the minds of everyone and everyone rallied round the Pope to guard his person and to help him in his needs.

At that minute two angels were seen carrying a standard who went towards the Pope saying 'Receive the standard of He who fought and dispersed the most powerful people on Earth. Your enemies will be defeated and your sons will shed tears and will call for your return with sighs.' Carrying the standard they could see that on one side was written *Regina sine labe concepta* (the Queen immaculately conceived) and on the other *Auxilium cristianorum* (the Help of Christians).

The Pope took the standard with joy, but gazed attentively at the small number of those who remained around him and became saddened by it. The two angels arrived saying: 'Go and console your sons. Write to your brothers spread around in various parts of the world, that it is necessary to make a reform in customs and in men. If it is not achieved the bread of the Divine Word will not be broken among the people. Catechise the young girls and preach detachment from the things of the Earth. The time is coming,' concluded the two angels, 'when the people will be evangelized by the people. The levites will be found among the hoes, the spade and the hammer, so that the words of David will come true: "God has raised up the people of the Earth to place on his throne the leaders of the people." '

When he heard this the Pope moved off and the length of the procession began to increase. When they began to set foot in the Holy City they wept for the desolation and for the citizens as so many of them were dead. They then re-entered St. Peter's intoning the Te Deum which was taken up by a choir of angels singing, 'Glory to God in the Highest and in Earth Peace among men of good will.' When the singing had come to an end, the darkness disappeared completely and a brilliant sun shone out.

The city, the countryside and the landscape were much denuded of population, the ground was churned up as if by a hurricane, a heavy shower and hail, and the people were arguing with spirit one against the other saying, 'God is in Israel.'

From the beginning of the exile until the singing of the Te Deum the sun will rise two hundred times. The whole time that will elapse while these things are completed will correspond to four hundred sunrises.

What Nostradamus Says about the Fate of the Papacy

At the time Nostradamus wrote about the Papacy, he had to take a great deal of care not to incur the very real wrath of the inquisitors who handed out punishments of prison or the stake. In contrast to what was believed at the time, this did not have a lasting effect on the power of the Popes. He predicted, rather, the end of the Papacy in unequivocal terms, when the fishing boat will be lost. (*Centuries* I, 4.)

For our study, excluding those things which have already come to pass, we will examine quatrains scattered through his works which we think refer to facts in the future, more or less close at hand. His work contains many clear and precise details about the fate of the Roman Papacy. The events forecast are essentially, schisms, birth of a new religion, transfer of the Roman Catholic Curia, the slaughter of priests and similar matters.

A Schism and Struggles for the Church

In the epoch before the apocalypse in which we live, do we not know of Marxist priests? If we meet any of them we call them atheists. Indeed, it is like the natives at the landing of Christopher Columbus, who not understanding the gold and the pearls they had, greedily preferred the pieces of glass and the mirrors which the dishonest Spaniards carried.

A sign of the times is the confusion which is already spreading everywhere. The abandonment of standards on the part of many is evident, by some in good faith but with little judgement. Enough people think of those who took seriously the French priest who proclaimed himself Pope with the name of Clement xv.

Before the great conflict and the invasion of the barbarians, revolutionary movements inside the Church will provoke a schism when the Pope dies. In fear that the little boat of St. Peter will sink many clergy will abandon the boat (*Centuries* ii, 57), throwing themselves out to swim alongside it. But because they were influenced solely by egotistic fear, they will be the first to drown. E. Ruir, in his commentary on Nostradamus, thinks the schism will take place in 1973 under the pontificate of *De Mediaetate Lunae*. If they do not agree about the dates, the agreement is, however, universal among all commentators about the events forecast.

According to viii, 20, when the conclave takes place, it will be confused:

The bogus message about the false elections, spread by the City, will end broken hopes, and capture the votes, the chapel will be tinted with blood and another weakening of the empire will take place.

There will be a period, according to some, in which the Church will be reduced to painful anarchy, as three Popes will be elected at the same time, an Italian, a Greek and a German and they will be enthroned by force of arms. These serious events, some declare, will take place after the present Pope, Paul vi, with the Pope *De Mediaetate Lunae*, or he who will follow afterwards. According to another prophecy (San Gioacchino 1200) the three will be killed and the Church remain a widow. There will always be struggles and contrasts, as x, 76 says:

The grand Senate (the conclave) will hail one of them

with ceremony, but he will be driven out afterwards. His supporters will be well acclaimed with the sound of the trumpet and the enemy expelled.

In addition to this, III, 65 says that the schismatic Pope, the Italian one, will be imprisoned and then killed. This is confirmed in IX, 99:

The wind from the North will blow the reeds apart while from the walls will be thrown ashes, lime and powder. The rain added to it will make things worse but at last help will come from the frontier.

The Pope will flee from Rome as a result of what will come from the North (the North Wind); the defence of Rome will provoke worse enemy reactions. The aid will be seen. But the woes will not seem over according to II, 57:

The great wall (which?) will fall, and the great one will be killed. His death will be unexpected and greatly regretted. The Ship being damaged, the greater part of the people will swim.... The ground near the river will be coloured with bloodstains.

Some prophets think that the true age of the Abomination will come when the seat of the Catholic Church is transferred. This event has been forecast by Nostradamus more times than by any other prophet. It seems that the 'Confusion of Israel' will have to last 153 months by our calendar as G. Barbarin points out in his book on the Great Pyramid.

Centuries VIII, 99 says: As a result of the power of the three temporal kings the Holy Seat will be transferred elsewhere, where the substances of the corporal Spirit will be replaced and received as the true Seat.

Only when the conflict is over will the Pope consent to return to his seat. The Church, as St. Bridget has written, will be trampled down. The church of St. Peter and the priesthood will fall into great danger. The church will be harried and driven out, but will not fall into slavery. According to V, 46; on the side of the red caps disputes and new schisms when the man from the Sabines is elected, there will be much specious argument

97

and Rome will be harmed by the Albanians.

This will be followed by an event exactly foretold in II, 41: The Great Star will shine out for seven days, a cloud will make two suns seem to appear, the great mastiff will howl all night when the Great Pontiff changes his territory.

Concerning the meaning of the circumstances which Nostradamus announces, at the same time as certain other events, one can only conjecture. Here is another example:

Alas a great people can be seen in torment and the holy law in complete ruin, all Christianity ruled by other laws, when a new mine for gold and silver will be found.

What is he talking about? Again, there is another mysterious circumstance forecast in VI, 66.

At the birth of the new seven the bones of the Great Roman badly buried will be found, the marble sepulchre will appear open; the Earth will quake in April.

The ship now appears in the power of the waves as *Centuries* V, 73 tells us: The Church of God will be persecuted and the holy temples despoiled, the mother will put a shirt on her naked son (when) the Poles and the Arabs are allied.

They are elements which will make themselves clear where the wrong comes from and how grave it will be and this is stressed in VIII, 98: The blood of the Churchmen will be spilled in great abundance like water and for a long time will not be dried up: look, look at the priesthood in ruins and groaning with pain.

Nostradamus affirms that the world will be put to sleep in its orgies, while the Pope will seek refuge in Avignon, because his own city will have already been captured. To say Avignon would mean exile because at the time of Nostradamus the period had already passed when the Pope had moved for a time to the French town. The struggle of the Church will affect everyone, but most of all its Head, who will carry the main burden as its scapegoat. A warning of this is given in II, 97: Roman Pontiff well guarded approaches the city watered by two rivers, you spit out your blood near to it, you and yours when the roses bloom.

After the death of the Pope *De Mediaetate Lunae* in 1987 a new Pope will be installed at Constantinople. Nostradamus confirms that he will be a Pope of French origin and with royal blood.

These events, preceded by the barbaric invasion, will submerge Germany, France, Spain and Italy. The Church, naturally, will be strongly hostile. Nostradamus goes so far as to say that the last Pope will be killed. But there will then be something good and new, a French Pope making plans for the renewal of the Church. This will bring about a spiritual change for the good.

As V, 79 says: The Sacred Pomp will lower its wings at the coming of the Great Legislator who will raise the humble, persecute the rebels, and on Earth no one will be born like him.

And from the East a Great Initiate will be seen who will bring a new light. X, 75: He who is awaited so expectantly will never return in Europe, but will appear in Asia one of the League brought up by the Great Hermit and later by all the Kings of Orient.

The Prophecies of St. Malachi about the Popes

When one talks of prophecies about the Popes one usually thinks of the man who goes under the name of St. Malachi, because he is best known and repeated. They are symbolic mottoes under which he names 112 Popes from Celestinus II (1143) until the last Pope of all. The motto has to be typical of the character of each one of them in chronological order and not distinguishing between Pope and Antipope. In 1595 a Benedictine monk, from the convent of St. Justin at Padua, Arnoldo de Wion, published in Venice a work entitled *Lignum Vitae*, dedicated to famous members of the Benedictine order. In this he reports the well-known prophecies about the Popes attributed to St. Malachi and following them with comments by a Dominican monk, F. A. Giaccomius.

Publication was delayed and the prophecies in it were fulfilled, giving cause for suspicion as it was written before the conclave in which lots were drawn for the election of cardinal Simoncelli di Orvieto, giving the motto which corresponds to 'Ex antiquitate Urbis' (Orvieto in Latin is 'Orbis Vetus') which was suitable for him. The Irish bishop, St. Malachi, to whom the prophecies are attributed, was a friend of St. Bernard of Chiaravalle. This man, in an autobiography which he wrote later, did not say directly that St. Malachi was the author of these prophecies, but refers to him as the maker of several prophecies which were fulfilled. The authenticity of the prophecies has been contested. But the arguments for and against their validity cancel each other out. But the truth of these prophecies is, in truth, only in their correctness.

We will relate those of them which refer to the Popes.

The Last Popes

The series of Popes will end with three Popes which the commentators call 'the Popes of the supreme tests'. They, after the present Pope, Paul VI, *Flos florum*, (The flower of flowers) are: (1) *De mediaetate Lunae* (from the middle of the Moon), (2) *De Labore suis* (from the work of the Sun), (3) *De gloria olivae* (from the glory of the olive). And then, at the end: In extreme persecution the Holy Roman Church was governed by Peter the Roman who looked after his flock in great trouble, which when it occurred destroyed the city of seven hills and a great judge pronounced upon his people.

Are we, therefore, very near the future?

Pius XII said in a discourse 'The Papacy is living because it is the stone of which the Church is built which lives for Christ and in Christ until the consummation of the centuries.' In the book *The Last Popes and the End of the World in the great Prophecies*, M. Dorato, commenting on this sentence of the Pontiff, writes: He seems to give credence to the prophecies of St. Malachi on the

Popes as this consummation of the centuries will not delay long in coming to pass. There are three Popes whose motto is preceded by *de*. But what is their real meaning? Each one has a symbol, the Moon, the Sun and the olive. We do not wish to take the place of the prophets but we wish to make hypotheses and conjectures.

(1) De Mediaetate Lunae. A schism? The Moon, as a symbol, represents the error in opposition to the sun which means the truth. Often, indeed it will mean an antipope. According to the Monk of Padua who called it *Saintly Mediators and Future Victims*, he would have to have the name of Pius XII, which was already taken by Cardinal Pacelli.

The Moon, in the latest adventures of Man, has taken its place in the newspapers. We do not know if in the symbols of St. Malachi it can refer to this sense.

For this Pope from the middle of the Moon, another interpretation is that he will see the Arab countries throw themselves on to Europe after the conquest of Palestine. This invasion will take on the character of a Holy War of Islam against the Christians. 'In 1973,' writes E. Ruir, 'the Mahometan hordes commended by the seventh Antichrist, will throw themselves on the European coast of the Mediterranean from Italy to Spain. It will not be, as was the Allied invasion of 1944, a landing at a chosen point, but an invasion of all the beaches which can be used by little landing ships (fishing boats, dinghies, or barges used in the open sea, small ships and the like). This invasion will succeed in setting foot on the defenceless coast as the population will be completely disarmed and the armed forces insufficient to cover such a front.' According to the same writer, Sicily and Sardinia will be the first objectives of the enemy. And he goes on : 'The dictatorial governments of France and Great Britain will have to send reinforcements to Italy to stop the invasion, but these reinforcements, after having fought at Genoa will have to retreat rapidly back into France.' The time of this pontificate is linked with the things Nostradamus has said. Thus, according to the aforementioned E. Ruir, it refers to an antipope, a religious renegade who persuaded the Christians of Italy to follow the new cult. 'The beast will talk like the Lamb and will imitate him,' is written in Revelations. The true Pope will be imprisoned and then deported into an Arab country where he will die. The seventh Antichrist, having overrun Italy and receiving reinforcements from Asia will overrun Austria, Hungary and Poland, then he will celebrate his victory and the Mahometan cult in the cathedral of St. Sophia in Constantinople. He will believe that he has fulfilled the wishes of Mahomet and transformed the crescent Moon into full Moon. For several years part of southern Europe will be occupied.

The Americans, surprised by these events, having broken off relations with a Europe ruined by revolution, will not take the initiative to intervene until the power of the Asiatics will menace them.

After the atrocities committed against the populace and the destruction of everything that is civilized, the Christians of America will force their governments to intervene. From Canada to Argentina they will take part in the struggle. The armies will disembark in Portugal, 'arming the Spaniards and chasing the Arabs from Spain. Their aircraft will parachute arms to the defenders of Europe and their fleet in the Mediterranean will destroy the convoys of arms and reinforcements of the Mahometan force. Then the hour of defeat will sound for Antichrist. Defeated in every sector, annihilated on the beaches where they landed, driven off the seas, then in North Africa which is rapidly overrun, they will be decidedly defeated in Palestine where the Arabs will not be able to remain.'

As the Mahometans will have ruined everything, the new Pope *De Labore Solis* will be installed, instead of at Rome, at Jerusalem.

(2) *De Labore Solis*. Will he work for the sun, for the triumph of the truth? There will be a period of peace. Then, perhaps, another conflict? The Monk of Padua

says that this Pope will be called Gregory XVII and his rule will be a time of expectation. But there was no Pope Gregory XVII, as the number was not assumed by him when he took office. According to P. Innocent Rissaut, this was the true *Pastor Angelicus*: Others call him the *Pastor Funalis* on account of his poverty. Some prophets think this will be the time the Jews are converted, others think this will take place in the last days under the following Pope.

(3) *De Gloria Olivae*. The glory of the olive is certainly the triumph of peace. The Monk of Padua attributed the name of Leo XIV to this Pontiff and calls his reign glorious. Everything seems to indicate a period of calm and quiet. But it is certain that the time which precedes the tempest is the more confusing.

(4) *Pietro Romano* (Peter the Roman). More than just the name of a person, it indicates a last epoch in contrast to that of Peter the Apostle who began it. The time of this Pope is that of the great tribulation which will end an era. He will be the Pope of the Apocalypse and will see the ruin of everything and the destruction of everything before complete renewal. The final Antichrist will enter the scene. People like E. Ruir, whose qualities we ignore as prophets and who dare to put dates to events they know nothing about, assign this period from 1995 to 2023, and assume, therefore, that in 1994 the eighth Antichrist will be absolute master of Asia and who will have caused the Sages of India to disappear from Tibet and will have forced the Mahometans so in terror to deny the Koran and recognize him as God, to whom everyone on Earth owes obedience. They will overcome the crowd by working wonders similar to miracles and everyone will prostrate themselves at their feet. Satan, the power for evil, will accord him all his negative power. He will undertake a war of extermination with 200 million combatants for the conquest of the Occident. They will be the long days of the new slavery and more tremendous, and they will be shortened for the love of the elect and will culminate in the Great Day.

It is the final act. Rome will disappear and the world will undergo the purification of fire.

But in the general destruction there will remain some who will see the new day, and the life will be revived, renovated for a new cycle.

The end of the Papacy will have no connection with the vitality of religion and the faith which is in the heart of every man. Institutions can change just as exterior manifestations of religion can take different forms. What cannot alter is the substance and no material force can ever touch it. Thus man rises in the road of life, this is how the feeling of religion penetrates man's mind and the external manifestations become more sophisticated by all members of present-day Humanity.

9

SAINTS AND SEERS, ASTROLOGERS AND SOOTHSAYERS

The coming of a New Age, religious, scientific and social has been foretold for a long time and we have been warned in anticipation the excitement of a changing life where one has the faculty of seeing the future, a thing which was then not understood and even laughed at by contemporaries. The fact that day succeeds day showing the completion of that which is invisible to the minds of man before it happens, was already understood.

The future fate of humanity has been written. We are the actors in the great drama.

From 1975 onwards

Many spiritual centres, small but flourishing groups, exist today in all parts of the world, and the various schools of an esoteric character announce that we are coming to a new age in the life of man and of the planet we inhabit.

Pius XII, on Easter Day, 1957, and the end of his Encyclical, exclaimed: Come, Lord Jesus, there are signs that your coming is not very far off ! ...

The theosophists affirm that the last twenty-five years of the century will have a very great importance. Great changes are seen with great consequences for humanity. Most of these men have learned from their Master that in the final quarter of the century evolution will take place at a much faster rate.

So as to precede and condition the Age of Aquarius, assert the wise men of the Arcana School, disciples of A. A. Bailey, interpreter of the thought of the Tibetan Master, attending the Land of the Initiates, their work will consist especially of acting as *avant-garde* of the

Old Men who will direct the evolution of humanity and in preceding them in external manifestations. They affirm the return of Christ to re-establish the divine plan on Earth. The work of the Initiates and their disciples up to 2025, will tend to produce fundamental changes in the thought, knowledge and life purpose of man; it is by nature revealing. The teaching will be given on a world scale with the most modern means such as radio, the press and television. During this time will occur the 'second precipitation,' as the Tibetans call it, 'and it will have to be consciously produced by humanity itself.' In order to help it a new Invocation will be given which will be amply spread about.

In human consciousness the divine idea will have to be born and gradually the awareness of a way of life and the Divine Plan will come. This is especially for the masses led astray and drunk with the false idea of happiness. These are the years for work during which those who have the higher vision of life will have to unite.

When Men have Developed their Civilization but cannot Improve Themselves

The Orientals affirm that everywhere in the last quarter of the century Humanity will be able to take advantage of help from Great Spiritual Beings who will play the part of the Hierarchy who direct the evolution of the world. Above all, in moments of great danger, such as the present time, such help can be at its greatest because it is most necessary.

In 1882, in the works of one of the Masters of Wisdom, the important warning was given of the march of humanity to self-destruction. This message was given in the book by A. P. Sinnet, *Esoteric Buddhism*:

The progress of Absolute Evil, which can only be stopped in a cataclysm, begins to show itself in every civilization which has reached its apogee, when, by means of purely intellectual research and ordinary scientific experiments, the men making up this race are rendered masters of particular powers over nature.

These powers are possessed by the Adepts but in the Adepts there is no evil, because they were acquired at the same time as the development of spiritual qualities; but in the hands of egoists and perverts they can become the most horrible instrument of crime.

When your race, which is the fifth, has reached the zenith of its physical intelligence, and has developed its civilization to the extreme and unable to advance further, its progress towards the absolute will be halted brusquely. In the same position the Lemurians and the Atlanteans were stopped in their progress and in their civilizations.

Thus in dependence on cyclic laws, which direct events, but which do not stop the action of individual wills, both causes and effects can be generated.

Where it is written (in the Bible) that sometimes a wise man is needed to save a city, and as a river at its origin has to flow round a stone, thus the will of the people, guided by a few can reach its terrible destiny which spreads out over humanity.

The Wonderful Jeane Dixon

In a book published in the U.S.A. and recently published in Italy in the same Italian series as the original Italian version of this book, *On the Threshold of the Future*, an extraordinary seer is written about, Jeane Dixon, who has given repeated proofs that she possesses the mysterious capacity of seeing into the future.

Her predictions are numerous, given out beforehand in clear language even in front of millions of spectators when taking part in programmes on television or local and national radio.

Mrs. Dixon is able to diagnose cases which doctors had not succeeded in recognizing; she can foresee events in people's personal lives before they happen. Famous instances of this were the deaths of Martin Luther King and Robert Kennedy. Notable predictions include the arrival of Communism in China, the launching of the first Sputnik, the re-election of President Truman and the assassination of President Kennedy. But her predictions were not always so accurate. Often the predictions of this American seer refer to events still in the future.

The seer told Rene Noorbergen her own story, revealing also what she expected for the future.

She writes 'Visions, telepathic messages, psychic sensations, have combined to give a deep realization of future events in our generation and when to announce these events, including those of cataclysms, which bring about great anxiety.'

What is more natural, when given the dramatic and even tragic nature of what is revealed in front of her eyes.

The Vicissitudes of Russia

The seer affirms the return of Russia to Christianity, not yet, but in a distant future, while today she is making a radical change in her way of life. The religious sentiment is so traditional and basic in these people, that 'it will be an integral part of a general rebirth of faith in Jesus Christ'.

Unfortunately, before this event, they will have to go through many tragic events, because Russia has the fixed plan to dominate the world, and to this end will use all methods with no exception at all, according to the cruel ideas of the men at the top who believe in nothing except brute material force. This 'grand design' will serve to stimulate the ignorant masses, and will penetrate the vital parts of every single state, with open subversion, prepared by a number of agents to try to create chaotic economic conditions in all other parts of every nation.

Special funds are set aside to support revolutionary movements among students and to make trouble between the races. Militant Marxists, who are directly dependent upon Russia, and professors who incite and then take part in student revolts, are the instruments, abeit unconscious, of this plan.

By 1980 there will be a notable increase in the weight of Russian power, exercised as well in the control and domination of the socialist world while at the same time there will be a great increase in the number of dictatorships controlled in different ways by the Russians.

The war will be almost the last one, and while it will be won by the democracies in the end, will cause divisions in the capitalist world as a result of the subtle and slow penetration, pressure and subversion which had been going on before.

All this activity and creation of disorder while seemingly independent and with the various movements even wishing to take control over each other by different degrees of extremism, are really controlled by various outside powers, but every occurrence has already been planned and is part of the plan of the central organization in Moscow, directed by three men who have the strings to pull in their hands, working out the details of their second plan.

The seer has seen 'with the eyes of the mind' that experiments in bacteriological warfare are being carried on in the confines of Russia and India. 'I have seen the end of thousands of flying objects while the war goes on. . . . The future will witness a war where the new arms can be tested. There will be a war costly in the losses of human life and of harvests.'

She writes also that the number of missiles destined for Western Europe will be about 750, hidden in the long chain of the Carpathian Mountains. While all the protagonists, the heads of the major countries, do not have any intention of disarming, the various conferences for world disarmament go on from year to year to quieten the people and to take away their sense of danger.

In Africa and Asia little fires of subversion and revolt

break out, fomented and encouraged also by Red China. Things will get progressively worse in Vietnam and in Korea. The facts will show that the treaty for the banning of nuclear experiments will be used to harm the United States and will hurt them very much.

The worsening of the world situation will lead to the breaking out of war in the decade 1980–90. Russia and the United States will be allied for a time against Red China. This war, despite enormous losses and sufferings, will provoke a spiritual renewal in humanity.

Before 1980 there will be a crescendo of little troubles, rebellions, rows between individuals, social classes, and nations outwardly friendly until it all becomes united in a huge flame of destruction.

The Drama of the New Generation

To forecast the future fate of generations which we can see quarrelling under our own eyes and claiming rights without admitting any corresponding duties, is absurdly easy. Jeane Dixon declares that by the preparation of the tragic events in the future, the generations who have to live through them will have to suffer much.

For many, salvation will come by studying psychic phenomena and extra-sensory perception, which will gain enormous popularity in the next ten years, while old preconceptions are discarded. Then people will carry out many experiments in all the psychic fields, and in the course of this road, many people will find their faith once more. Indeed, these phenomena will kindle the light of spirituality in many people.

From 1979, according to the seer, there will be a series of food crises because all the technical knowledge and resources will be increasingly used in the conquest of space, instead is turning round and solving the problems of the Earth, which is the real mother of everything Men can attain and can produce for their own physical life.

In addition to this, an economic struggle of gigantic proportions will break out between the West and Japan, which thanks to its constant progress will become one of the greatest economic powers in the world.

A Comet will Menace the Earth

'Towards the middle of 1980' Mrs Dixon declares 'the Earth will be struck by a comet. Earthquakes and tidal waves will be the result of this tremendous collision which will take place in one of the great oceans. It will be one of the worst disasters of the twentieth century. Although the approximate point of impact has already been revealed to me, I believe that I should not reveal it yet, but at a future date I will give more detailed information.'

And is this, perhaps, the first of the cosmic cataclysms of nature, forecast by many people, among which are many inspired prophetic messages, which come from various sources?

Earthquakes and tidal waves have been forecast in many other prophecies with effects on human life which are easy to imagine. But what would happen after a collision with a comet would suggest a disaster of cosmic proportions.

The same Jeane Dixon declared that another calamity which she did not define would take place after this one a few years later. 'Towards the half-way mark in the 1980s, and particularly around 1985 Nature will interfere in a direct manner in the plans by Russia for world conquest. Indeed, in that year a natural phenomenon will take place which will profoundly change the events which will influence the course of humanity.'

Even now, many sceptics and doubters are turning away from Christ, and many things will be changed. But indeed, strangely enough, when all this is over, it will seem to some people as if it had never happened at all. These will be those with closed minds, who, although being affected, will blind themselves in their primitive way owing to their lack of evolution and shut themselves off from any effect. When the events are repeated these people begin to think for thmselves until maturity is reached and their minds can rise to a more stable plane where there is light and greater progress.

China Against Russia

According to the seer, China will be the greatest danger in future. After all the preceding struggles, in the first quarter of the twenty-first century, China will show its teeth.

'In 2025 China will have achieved sufficient economic and political stability to launch a plan of great conquest. In that year China will invade Russia and conquer a large part of the north of that country and they will not stop until they have invaded Finland, Norway, Sweden and Denmark, stopping at the German border.

'Western Europe will not be invaded then, Russia, too, will have enlarged her sphere of influence by then and it will not be limited to the countries of Eastern Europe but will extend to Libya, Ethiopia, Iran and a great part of Africa.

'This war of conquest will last from 2025 to 2037.'

The rivalry between China and Russia is the hostility of two giants. The conflict will assume vast dimensions making the previous struggles seem small in comparison. The vast horde of arms collected in the Middle East, North Africa, South Africa and in countries like Venezuela, Bolivia and Guatemala, will be put into use.

Arabs and Israelis

The seer saw nothing but woe in the Middle East. 'A true peace is a very long way ahead in time. The discord will come to an end after Jerusalem has been destroyed by an earthquake.'

There will, therefore, be constant tension, diplomatic

activity, battles on and off, the occasional truces, but endless ferment.

But there will be worse to come. About 2000 there will be an invasion of Chinese and Mongols with a battle taking place to the east of Jordan. It is a war between East and West. The scales will be tipped heavily against Israel but the Orientals will suffer great losses and Israel will not be beaten.

With this bellicose period over, Israel will become stronger and richer, but its people will credit divine aid and nothing else, and will at last recognize Jesus Christ as Son of God.

Scientific and Technical Progress

Amidst so much fighting and ruin caused by the wars, invasions, and natural cataclysms on top of hardships which are unexpected and due to hunger, Man will be forced to use his own initiative to survive. 'And then,' wrote the seer, 'there will be discoveries in the field of medicine which will control Man's health, his economy and the whole system of living.'

The oceans will become the mines from which many necessary foods will be obtained. Discoveries in the field of propulsion will be made and cosmic magnetic forces will be used which will allow space flights between the planets with unbelievable ease.

But, what is more important, many men will rediscover comradeship in adversity and will realize that the only way is that of love, a thought which will be repeated over and over again in many messages of a prophetic and inspired nature.

The Vicissitudes of the Church

For the Catholic Church the seer foresees drastic changes for the next twenty years, both in the doctrinal field and in that of tradition. The Church will find itself divided not only in questions of dogma or principle, but of discipline and morale.

'The ecumenical movement which so many expect,' says the seer, 'will unfortunately be a sign deprived of consistency and devoid of real meaning. I see more disturbances in the various churches in the present century than in the previous one. The next 29 years will be ones of struggles and divisions.'

Sects and factions will arise with views which will cancel each other out. Many priests will marry and do other things against the rules, creating diversions and troubles without precedent.

But the majority of people will remain faithful to the oldest traditions.

'A divine intervention' writes the seer 'will show itself at the end of the century when a cross will appear in the eastern sky and a loud voice will call men to unite under one God. Although now in divided churches, men will be called to unite in the same catholic faith.

'In the dramatic ups and downs towards the end of the century one Pope will be wounded and another killed. This Pope will be one elected by only a few people, and his election will be disputed and not gain the approval of the leading Roman churchmen. But he will have such power that the strength of the opposition will melt away before him.'

'This Pope will be the last one to govern the Church on his own,' says Jeane Dixon, because the cardinals will enjoy ever-increasing power until they take on the right of changing a Pope whom they do not like.

The Sinister Figure of the Liar

But the person who takes most of the attention of Jeane Dixon is the sinister image of the Liar, who is revealed in the Protean aspect of the deceiver. On Antichrist, his predecessors, his doctrine and his followers, Mrs. Dixon has extremely clear and precise words, which are worthwhile reading in the text.

As prologue to his base deeds, indulging in occult and

abominable acts, we see this addict of Satan already carrying out various forms about which the chronicles are also full.

'Satan is advancing with his discoveries to seduce the world and we must prepare ourselves for future events.

'His sphere of action is the individual seduction of humanity, by an ideology which is a mixture of political, philosophical and religious concepts, which will throw the faith of men in God into great confusion.

'While the prophet of Antichrist will propound his ideology, men will be dazzled by technical progress and the opulence of their way of living. Society will end up by worshipping itself and its material progress. At last the moment will come when Man will say "I am the power in the world and have no need of God. I only need my own Human science."'

Before the coming of the false Christ, his propaganda and his followers will proclaim his 'fearful and terrifying despotism destined to be exercised in all parts of the world'.

Then will be performed the 'miracles' whose wonderful achievements 'they will carry out on the mistaken roads of the inhabitants of the Earth'. What will be more convincing will be the conquest of the forces of nature, of which the 'fire from the sky' will be the most important symbol. All these things will not be supernatural, but products derived from the conquest of human science, but they will be interpreted in such a way as to take men further from God and direct them towards the cult of Antichrist.

Besides, the false scientific prophet will cause a proud and conceited spirit to grow up in the science of Antichrist which will render many religious traditions outdated and unacceptable to men of that age who will call the period 'illuminated'.

We should try and think of this science which many men will adore.

The rejection of God and atheist thought that the

false prophet is the only source of knowledge and wisdom.

They will promise to make the reign of justice be born on Earth, offering a complete liberation to the human race, adding the prospect of unity, solidarity, peace and happiness among men.

This is the language of all those who dally with so much evil and proclaim themselves liberators.

But what do they give? How can they give something which they have not got themselves?

Antichrist has already been Born in the Middle East

In a vision in February 1962 Jeane Dixon told how she had had the revelation of an extraordinary event: the birth in a certain place in the Middle East shortly after seven in the morning of 5 February 1962 of a baby who will revolutionize the world, who will create a false Christianity based on his 'omnipotence' and who will lead men along a road very far from the teaching of Christ.

'The circumstances of his birth and the events that I have seen, makes his life very like that of Christ, nevertheless so different that I have never had any doubt at all that this child will be no other than the Antichrist who will deceive the world in the name of Satan.'

His life seems to be an imitation of that of Christ. 'I see that he is no longer in the country in which he was born but has been taken by his parents into another place in the Middle East, and I have a distinct impression that it is a thickly populated zone of the United Arab Republic.

'The reason for his removal is unknown to me, but I know that the child is surrounded by forces working for his protection.

'When this child reaches the age of eleven something tremendously important will happen. Most probably at that time (1973–4) nothing at all will be made public, but he at that age, will come to realize the full import of his satanic mission.

'He will then begin to extend his influence, and those who are nearest to him will form the first circle of loyal supporters when he reaches 19 years of age. He will devote himself silently to his work together with his supporters until he is around 29 or 30 at the time when the force and impact of his presence in the world will begin to harvest its evil fruits.'

The influence of this man will begin to be felt by the end of 1980, but it will increase steadily, and his doctrines will spread, making use of the propaganda machine of the United States, which it will use for its cause as something that is indispensable. He will make, in addition to this, frequent journeys in North America, in order to obtain the close co-operation, which he has already offered to the American government. The power of this man will increase greatly until 1999. By this time every type of religious instruction will have almost disappeared from schools and the youth of that day will prove easy to ensnare in doctrines which are diffuse. The young will contribute much to this doctrine, taking power in the world.

Those who have not changed their Christian principles will be thrown into confusion by this evil doctrine.

The Worst Tyranny

Jeane Dixon declares that Antichrist will, in essence, be a phenomenon of ordinary politics. The world will neglect a religious heretic, but cannot ignore anyone with great power to use as an instrument for his own ends.

'He will be a military figure. He will conquer the world and know how to hold it to subjection by force of arms.

'His domination will extend to the whole world and to every individual person, controlling even their thoughts. There will be no individual states any more and the whole world will become a great island in the universe. War, as it has always been known, will come to an end, and Antichrist will proclaim himself 'the Prince of peace'.

'For many members of the Christian church there will seem to be no way out and in the end the Church will be reduced to a clandestine organization. Nothing will remain of its original position in the world, but the Holy Spirit will follow and help its members just as Christ said "even unto the end of the world".'

But she goes on to tell us more:

'He will establish a "religion" which is foreign and fundamentally anti-human, based on atheism and on the struggle against all forms of religion.'

This is the beast that Christian tradition identifies with Antichrist. The typical traits also appear that identify the beast for us (1) the domination of Man with an iron hand; (2) the seduction of the minds of men by a false doctrine put in by propaganda.

'It is presented to the human race as a supreme controller who is able to remove every trace of war, as master of the new way of life which moves away from the Christian tradition, already considered out of date and as "redeemer" of all men from their past poverty, their guilt complexes and mutual dislike and distrust.

'Antichrist will represent a profound ethical challenge to the men of his time, forcing them even to admit his "sanctity" over human life and culture. And all this will be nothing else than the result of atheism.

'This dishonest demoniac who will impose himself on men in those days will have two components (1) a false ideology, inculcated into everyone by means of a subtle propaganda; (2) mysterious and wonderful signs.

'As a result of his influence and teachings there will be universal confusion, divisions and schisms. Any religion which wishes to acclaim atheism and the few faithful who retain the conviction that there is only one God, will be bound to suffer great violence and all because of the works of him who is considered "the Prince of Peace".'

The Prophecy of the Flowering Almond Tree

In the spring of 1944 a certain Nicol Rycempel found in the ruins of the Church of St. Paul in Berlin, a manunscript contained in a tube of lead. This turned out to be the prophecy of a Benedictine monk of the early nineteenth century. Among other things it announced the death of the crooked lion (Hitler) before the thirteenth flowering of the Almond tree. It was then wartime and Germany was being hammered by bombardments and reduced to a heap of rubble. The hope of bringing this torment to an end raised the hopes of all as the thirteenth flowering corresponded to the spring of 1945. These prophecies circulated among the Germans for a couple of years and the police had orders to find them at all costs. Because of this the manuscript was hidden away.

As with other prophecies, one cannot be sure of the authenticity of this one. The good point about it is the way in which the events are forecast accurately year by year from 1900 onwards. Here are those which refer to future years:

1972	Triumph of the pilot.
1973	Light in the night.
1974	Road of the stars.
1975	Storm of the crosses.
1976	Love of the Moon.
1977	Terrestrial dizziness.
1978	Forbidden dreams.
1979	Death of Judah.
1980	Rome without Peter.
1981	Triumph of Work.
1982	The New Man.
1983	Hosanna by the people.
1984	Ravings in Space.
1985	The voice of Antichrist.
1986	Fire from the Orient.
1987	Glade of crosses.

1988 Madness on Earth.
1989 Expectation by men.
1990 A sigh in the sky.
1991 Light in the darkness.
1992 Fall of the stars.
1993 Death of Man.
1994 Roar of a wild beast.
1995 Sob of the mother.
1996 Flood on Earth.
1997 Death of the Moon.
1998 Glory in the Skies.
1999 The new Peter.
2000 Triumph of the olive.

There has been a commentary on these prophecies. They are for the most part exercises of fancy but they do have the signs of being made by a prophet who is able to foretell the truth. We have said several times that the exact dates do not matter, but only the events which can take place a little while before or afterwards. The Abbess of Rupertsberg, given the name of St. Hildegarde, although she has never been canonized, was the authoress of many prophecies. Her revelations have become classics. In *Scivias*, where she describes the end of the world, and in her apocalyptic visions, she recommends us not to look for the hour when these events will take place.

Saints and Seers

Among the Saints it is a common phenomenon to see and feel things which escape the ordinary mortal. And it is natural that it should be so, they have, more than other people, the custom of feeling and seeing in a dimension unknown to others. Thus in their lives, we read of extraordinary things happening which the sceptics deny as they do not understand them.

In the visions of Saints and in the various apparitions of religious characters, it is often the case that seers and sensitives say they have seen Jesus Christ who shows Himself angered by men, of the Madonna saddened by the conduct of men today. Certainly emotions and passions are not things that a very highly developed being could have. But this is language adapted to be understood by the speaker and which is also wrapped up in emotions and passions. The same thing is done when small children are being taught who do not understand any other type of language.

It is also evident that all the Christian prophets have been influenced by reading the sacred texts, particularly the Old Testament, where the wrath, scorn and the revenge of Jehovah, who cast lightning and punishments, was the way to rule the primitive Jewish people, still unable to understand any other sort of language, least of all love.

Today we realize that the coming of a new human cycle will bring the necessary changes which are also sad.

Jesus brought love. And everything that happens is for the good, just as love is a surgical operation; if indeed sad, it is dedicated solely to the love of the cure.

According to St. Augustine we are at the 'sixth period' of the human story, which goes from the birth of Jesus until the end of time. He wrote that in the last days all the Nations will run to the house of the Lord.

But as for anticipating when this time will be, St. Hildegarde says: Man should not know when the world will come to an end because the Father has kept this secret to Himself. Despite this, the same prophetess declared that between 1955 and 1980 the Earth will be the theatre for actions of various Antichrists. Jasper von Dortmund, a peasant living in the eighteenth century, and recognized by all the prophets, said:

I fear that war will come from the east and it will be so fast that in the evening it will be peacetime and in the morning the enemy will be at the gate. It will not be peace, it will not be a war of religion as all believers will make common cause together. The signs of this war will be: half-hearted religious feelings and corruption of customs, vice will be called virtue, and virtue, vice. Believers will be thought mad and unbelievers for those who have received the true light. Then the enemy will appear in large numbers exterminating everything. Battles, victory and flight will take place so rapidly that one will only have to hide for a short time to escape the danger. He who does not hide will be killed. The Turks will, at this moment, be our ally but later they will be defeated so severely that few will return to their own country.

P. Innocent Rissaut reports as well the prophecy of an unknown German seer a few centuries ago:

God will chastise the world: from the East and from the North a stubbornly-fought war will break out on all sides, with the hordes of barbarians flooding the country as far as the Rhine. But in the depths of our misery God will send a Saviour from the land of sunshine (Italy).

Another ancient prophecy repeats that: The people of the North will win at first, but then their power will be broken.

Similarly Anna Katherine Emmerich (1824), the great Augustine mystic had a vision of Antichrist working about 1960.

A monk of Olivet from the thirteenth century has said that between 1955 and 1980 the Abomination of Desolation will have reigned. St. Brigit also declared that the impious would prevail until 1980. In a revelation of the Madonna to Berthe Petit in Belgium in 1943 the following was said:

'The punishments will approach like clouds which increase in size and spread out so as to cover everything; sparks will spread everywhere which will annihilate the people in fire and in blood. What a terrible prospect! The Heart of the Virgin would despair if she did not know at what point the Divine Justice will have to intervene for the salvation of the minds and the purification of the people.' And on another occasion the same Berthe Petit said:

'Humanity is approaching a fearful torment, which will divide the people, reduce the human alliance to nothing, will show that nothing lasts except Me and I am He who directs the destiny of the people. That is the moment to give yourself completely to the Immaculate Heart of Mary.'

On 21 January 1868, the venerable Philomena de Santa Colomba, a nun in the monastery of Vals in Catalonia, wrote:

'There are four years that I see which will be terrible with the calamities and punishments which will menace the world: it will be like another flood, not of water but of a thousand other calamities ... Nevertheless, I had, on the other hand, the consolation of knowing that the Heart of Jesus will come out like a river of abundant grace which will once again fertilize the Christian world, and which will bring with it the triumph of the Church.'

Jean Le Royer had an ecstatic vision of the end of the world which from a number of deductions will take place around 2000 after the disappearance of the last Pope.

Three days of darkness

The blessed Anna Maria Taigi announced in 1837:

'I see above the Earth the immense darkness which will last for three days and three nights. Nothing will be visible and the air will be harmful and pestilential and will vomit harm, but not exclusively to the enemies of religion. During these three days, artificial light will be impossible, only sacred candles will burn. During this alarm, the faithful should stay in their houses and recite the Rosary and give Misericords to God. All the enemies of the church, both visible and unknown, will perish on Earth during this universal darkness, except those few who are converted to elect a new Pope.'

Marie Julie Jahenny de la Faudais in 1819 announced similar phenomena with equal precision:

'There will be three days of continual darkness. During

this fearful darkness only the candles which have been blessed will burn. One candle will last for three days, but in the houses of the impious they will not burn. During these three days demons will appear in horrible and nauseating forms and will make the air resound with appalling blasphemies. Rays and flashes will penetrate the houses of men but will not conquer the light of the blessed candles, which will be extinguished neither by winds nor by torments and earthquakes. A red cloud like blood will traverse the sky, the rumble of thunder will make the Earth tremble. The sea will reverse in foamy waves upon the Earth. Indeed, our planet will become one huge cemetery. The bodies of the impious as with those of the just will cover the soil. The desolation which will follow will be enormous; all the vegetation of the Earth will be destroyed as also will be the greater part of mankind. The crisis will come on suddenly and the disaster will be universal.'

In 1878 La Soeur Marie de Jésus Crucifié of Pau had a vision which probably confirms the earlier prophecy:

'During the three days of darkness, those who walk along their paths of deprivation will perish, in which way only the fourth part of humanity will survive.'

St. Gaspare de Bufalo, founder of the Congregation of the Most Precious Blood, also foresaw in 1837 this terrible catastrophe:

'Those who survive the three days of darkness and of weeping will appear to themselves as the only survivors on Earth, for in truth the world will be covered with bodies.'

The prophecy of St. Odilia

It is remarkable that St. Odilia foresaw the recent Second World War in details of time and in its description of the series of defeats and victories. We repeat here only those concerning future time:

'Woe to those who, in those days, do not fear the Antichrist, for he is the father of those who are repelled by crime. He will arouse still more homicides and many people will shed tears over his evil customs. Men will set themselves one against the other and at the end will want to re-establish order. Some will try to do this but will not succeed and thus will end up even worse off than before! But if things will have reached the summit and if the hand of man can no longer do anything, it will be put in the hands of Him, who will send down a punishment so terrible that it will not have been seen before. God has already sent the Flood, but He has sworn never to send one again. What He will do will be something unexpected and terrible. But the age of peace under the steel will have arrived, and the two horns of the Moon will become a cross. In those days frightened men will adore God in truth, and the sun will shine with an unusual brilliance.'

The Vision of Elisabetta Canori

On 10 December 1815 Elisabetta Canori had a vision: she saw the Church in the form of a venerable old woman, beautiful and covered with rich ornaments, but full of sadness, who cried to God in ardent supplication for her unfortunate sons. The Lord said to her:

'Pay attention to My justice and judge your own cause yourself.' Then she paled and began to divest herself of all her ornaments. Behold three angels carrying out a divine decree began to strip her of her vestments of glory. The venerable old woman, reduced to a humble state, felt that her strength was leaving her and swayed almost to the point of falling. The Lord did not permit this, but gave her a new vigour and set the cap of an illustrious matron on her head, who saddened and quite downcast at being abandoned by her sons, seemed to be in a profound darkness. Then the Lord surrounded her with his glory and passed on to her something of His splendour; she sent out powerful rays of light to the four cardinal points of the compass, completing wonderful miracles. The inhabitants of the Earth, dazzled by the splendour of the light, and as if wakened from a profound dream, got up, and leaving the darkness of their error, ran towards the light of the Gospel, confessing the faith of Christ and casting themselves down in complete repentance before the illustrious Lady who appeared more beautiful and more glorious than before.'

These revelations caused an internal struggle to arise in the mind of Elizabeth. She wished to see the triumph, but shied away from the thought of the flagellation which would have to precede it, praying that the Lord would take her from it, and to spare her from this mortal anguish. Later on the Lord told her openly that the triumph of the Church would be preceded by a terrible punishment and the annihilation of the impious, and then the blood of martyrs would freely flow. (*Biography*, Chapter xxvii.)

A Little White Cloud between the Two Towers of Santa Maggiore at Rome

The venerable P. Bernardo M. Clusi, monk of the order of Minors of S. Francesco da Paola, declared that there would come a time of general perversion and the world would become very bad indeed. He said: When I think of it the hair stands up on my head. The Lord has made known to me many times that the Devil was where he could do no harm. He spoke in this manner also to the nuns of Baby Jesus on Mount Esquiline and added:

'Not you yourselves, but those of your sisters who will be there when it happens, will be the first to perceive the great thing which God will do in putting the world in a state of peace, for it will start by the appearance of a little white cloud between the two campaniles of S. Maria Maggiore. And this great event, at the same moment that it will be visible in Rome, will indeed be visible also in the whole world. Then also the most hardened sinners will be converted, lowering their heads and beating their breasts saying "This is indeed the work of the Hand of God."

'And, a little time afterwards, the world will be like Paradise as anticipated, everyone will be so secure that when he goes out of his house he will be able to leave the door open freely as no one will go inside.'

Paracelso has predicted that at the end of time there would be a discovery of how to change metals, which is not clearly defined. Some people think that this refers to the discovery of atomic fission.

An unknown German monk, living in the seventeenth century seems to be the author of a prophecy which Ludwig Emmerich reports in his book, *Die Zukunft der Welt* (The Future of the World). It says:

'The 20th century will be a period of terror and misery. In that century everything evil and disagreeable that can be imagined will happen. In many countries the princes will rise up against their fathers, the citizens against authority, the children against their parents, the pagans against God, entire peoples against the established order. A civil war will break out in which bombs will fall from heaven. And then a further one will break out in which almost all the world will be turned upside down. Financial disasters and ruin of property will cause many tears to fall. Men will be without mind and without piety. Poisonous clouds and rays which can burn more deeply than the equatorial sun, iron armies marching, flying vessels full of terrible bombs and of arrows, fatal flying stars and sulphuric fire destroying great cities. This century will be the most perverse of all because men will raise themselves up and destroy each other mutually.'

The nun Bertine Bouquillon, a nurse at the Hôpital de St. Loius at St. Omer in northern France, who died with the reputation of a saint in 1850, predicted that:

'The end of time is near and Antichrist will not delay his coming. We shall not see him and not even the nuns who will follow him, but those who will come later will fall under his domination. When he comes nothing will be changed, in the nunnery everyone will be dressed as usual, the religious exercises and the services will go on as usual ... when the sisters will realize that Antichrist is in charge.'

Bartholomaus Holtzhauser, who died in 1658, said that Antichrist would reveal himself at the age of $55\frac{1}{2}$ years. Others said that, on the other hand, he would be about 30, thus imitating the actions of Christ.

Salvaneschi speaks of an American seer, Mary, who had foretold, in 1930, that the Antichrist had already been born in Jerusalem. His father is a bishop and his mother a nun of Jewish origin. In another revelation she announced that the Antichrist, already alive, was an ordinary man who belonged to Judah. His personality will be revealed in 1958. In addition, just as with Nostradamus, and with the Protocols of Savi, the supreme council of Sion, Mary too prophesies the fall of the Vatican at the hands of an Antipope. Then Lucifer will give himself a material body to appear as a man in the midst of other men. According to Mary, Antichrist will die around 1980.

The visions of Sister Elena Aiello

Very clear predictions on times to come are attributed to the Sister Elena Aiello, the holy nun, well-known for having warned Benito Mussolini without success about all the disasters which would come to Italy if she entered the war on the side of Hitler.

'An impious propaganda has spread many errors through the world, causing persecution, ruin and death everywhere. If men do not stop offending my Son the time will not be far off that the Justice of the Father will inflict upon Earth the whip it deserves, and the punishment will be worse than has ever been seen in the story of Man. When an extraordinary sign appears in the sky men will know that the punishment of the world will be soon!' (7 January 1950).

'I wish you to know that the whip is near; fire, never before seen, will rain down on the Earth and the greatest part of humanity will be destroyed. This time will be desperate for the impious, with cries and satanic blasphemies they will cry out to be covered by the mountains and will try and take refuge in caves, but it will be in vain. . . .

'Those who remain will find the misericord of God in my protection, while all those who do not wish to repent of their sins will perish in a sea of fire. Blessed are those in that time who can claim to be the true followers of the Virgin Mary.

'Russia will be almost completely burned up. Other nations will disappear as well. Italy will be saved in part by the Pope.' (11 April 1952).

'The world has sunk down into extreme corruption . . . Those who govern have become true devils incarnate, and while they talk of peace, they get ready more powerful armies . . . to destroy people and nations. (16 April 1954.)

'The anger of God is near and the world will be struck by great calamity, bloody revolution, strong earthquakes, famines, epidemics and tremendous hurricanes which will make the rivers and sea overflow! The world will be convulsed with a new and terrible war! Deadly armies will destroy nations, peoples and the things they love. In this sacrilegious struggle, as a result of the fierce driving power and bitter resistance, much will be hurled down of what has been made by the hand of Man. The dictators on Earth, real infernal monsters, will hurl down the churches with their Sacred Food (for Holy Communion and the Mass). Clouds bright with fire, will suddenly appear right across the sky and a storm of fire will beat down on all the world. This terrible scourge, never before seen in human history, will last for seventy hours. The impious will be reduced to powder and many will be lost in the obstinacy of their sins. Then the power of the light will be seen above the power of darkness.' (16 April 1955).

From the message of 1959: 'There will be a great duel between Myself and Satan ... Materialism will advance speedily in all nations and continue its progress leaving a trail of blood and death! . . .

'If Man does not turn to God, a great war will be seen from the east and from the west, a war of terror and death, and at the end purifying fire will fall from the sky like flakes of snow on all the people and a great part of the human race will be destroyed.'

'Russia will march on all the nations of Europe, particularly on Italy and will fly her flag on the cupola of St. Peter's.'

'The world has become an alluvial valley which is filled up with detritus and mud! I will be still in the power of the hardest test of divine Justice before the infernal flame burst out on all humanity. . . .

'Great calamities will be seen in the world, which will bring confusion, tears and sadness for all. Great earthquakes will submerge towns and countries. Epidemics and famine will bring terrible destruction, especially where the sons of darkness are to be found. Never has the world in this tragic hour more need of prayer and penitence, because the Pope, the church and the priests are in danger, as Russia will march on Europe, and especially on Italy, with much ruin and desolation. . . . Those who govern will not understand this because they will not have the true Christian spirit and are also blind in their souls, as they do not understand the truth. In Italy, too, they will be like ravening wolves dressed in sheepskins, because while they call themselves Christians they will open the door to materialism, making dishonest customs flood the country and bring Italy to ruin, but many of them will go in confusion. . . .

'My prediction for Italy will be shown, as it will be spared the fire, but the sky will be covered with very dark clouds and the Earth will shake with awesome earthquakes, which will open up deep chasms, and will also destroy cities and provinces; and all will cry out that it is the end of the world!

'Rome too will be punished according to justice because of its many and great sins, because scandal has arrived at its peak. The good, however, who suffer and those persecuted because they believe in justice and fairmindedness, will not have to fear, because they will be separated from the impious and the obstinate sinners and will be saved!'

This is the final message of 22 August 1960:

'Humanity has moved away from God, and, concentrating on the good things of this world has forgotten the heavens and if he has been corrupted very deeply he will not escape when the time of the flood comes! ... But the hour of the justice of God is near and it will be terrible! Tremendous scourges will afflict the world and many countries will be struck by epidemics, famine, earthquakes, great hurricanes and death! ... And if men do not repent under these scourges to reach for the Divine Misericord and do not return to God with a speed that is truly Christian, another terrible war will break out in the East and West, and Russia, with its secret armies will fight America, conquer Europe and the river Rhine in Germany especially will be seen full of corpses and of blood.

'Italy, too, will be struck with a great revolution and the Pope will suffer greatly. The enemy, like a roaring lion, will advance on Rome, and its jaundiced hatred will poison peoples and nations. . . .'

10

PROPHETIC AND INSPIRED MESSAGES

> *No unbeliever would understand, but the faithful will understand.* The Prophet Daniel.

Those who study and research into things to come, will know that certain events will take place in the near and distant future – indeed the preparation is already taking place. In various messages we have found the same warnings with a significant similarity to the prophetic announcements of clairvoyants. In many communications as well, which are all part of psychic experience, it has been proved that many transmissions have been inspired by the highest light. Some sensitives are true aerials of stations which receive and pick up messages which are invisible to men who are too blind and deaf to receive them. This was one of the messages that were received in this way in the past:

'And it shall come to pass in the last days, saith God, I will pour out of my Spirit upon all flesh: and your sons and your daughters shall prophesy, and your young men shall see visions and your old men shall dream dreams.' (Acts 2 : 17.)

The contacts with the invisible are among the most beautiful things in existence when they serve to point out the right path among wayward humanity and act as a way to find a higher spiritual life.

The Entities affirm that the Earth is inhabited mostly by inferior beings in total ignorance of the Divine Plan, who believe that they are the highest in the scale of life, and only because they even believe that nothing exists on a higher level than they do. Only a few were highly evolved. This produces a very unstable equilibrium and causes all sorts of troubles. But in the plan of the Grand Life, the Earth is only a stage in the long road of development of living beings. Now is just the time to make a selection among men to find those who are more mature, those worthy of moving on to a higher grade.

The Entities themselves affirm, moreover, that the present epoch corresponds to that which is called the 'Epoch of the Beast' in the Book of Revelation, that is the age of base passions and materialism. The '666' would represent the end of the third of the five great cycles of evolution, each of which is indicated by the figure 6 in esoteric symbolic language.

They affirm besides, that in the second half of our century, there will be increasing preparation for the change of cycle, while the confusion becomes ever more violent with electro-magnetic storms, cataclysms and earthquakes. The Earth itself will change it shape getting longer in the North–South direction by a special phenomenon of 'breathing' along its axis.

The transition from one cycle to another will not be sudden but will take place over centuries. 'Count up to three of them,' has been said. And then there will surely be apocalyptic events. In this epoch a rain of fire will come down on almost every region on Earth. It really should be the final epoch.

Action on a large scale will begin in South America where there will be a break in the surface of the Earth which will alter the present geocentric equilibrium of the terrestrial globe. This will have as a result the submerging of all America which will give Atlantis a chance to rise once more.

Because men can make themselves able to endure outstanding changes in the atmosphere, there will be changes in the organic make-up of Man. There will be other changes in his social and economic conditions overthrowing the barriers between men and nations. Every change brings suffering, but only sacrifice creates opportunities. By this way alone can man receive the impulse to rise up to the new plane of life.

We will give some samples of these prophetic and inspired messages coming from various centres.

A Luminous Aurora

An aurora will rise up which will reflect the splendour, the colour and the light of the Father. This aurora will be very near and will heat and illuminate everything and everyone. Its luminous gilded twilight can be glimpsed already and the emanation of heat will take place when the Father comes. It will join together all humanity which works, gets tired, sweats and which has blood flowing through its veins; on that humanity which is the favourite of the Son, who came down on Earth to save and redeem it; that humanity has laboriously travelled along the road to its own Calvary, but directed on high and in the heaven towards the Father, from whom flow out strength, brightness and heat to follow their way to perfection and to redemption.

Albano, 2 April 1962.

Men of Today

Humanity today is worse than in the time of Niniveh whom Jonah came to warn before its punishment. For that reason the expiation today should be greater than that in the time of Niniveh, whose people made true penitence and so escaped destruction.

From Akademiestrasse 15, Munich.

The Sign of the Cross will Shine out Brightly in the Sky

... and all men will tremble as if they were facing Eternity, repenting of their sins and making a solemn profession of faith. There will be a great miracle of the universal confusion for the purification of the world from all iniquity ... God will come upon sinful Earth with a terrible noise in a roaring tempest on a cold and dark winter's night. Hailstones of a size never before seen and lamps of fire will devastate, burn and incinerate everything that is dominated by sin, pride, dishonesty and the audacious folly of Man. Furthermore the ground and the trees will shake and everyone will expect the end of the world, but it will not be the end, on the contrary, it will be the beginning of the Justice of God . . .

At the tremendous roll of thunder you will have to close the doors and shutter windows so as to hide completely the light from without so that you cannot profane with your curiosity, the holy anger which will purify the Earth for the Just and for the small flock who remain faithful to him. . . . Then you will hear the voices of persons dear to you, not clearly because they are not those people but demons who by deception are trying to enter your house. Pray instead to the spirit returned to God before the Crucifix and put yourself in prayer under my cloak of the holy Mother of God with faith and without fear. If you know how to fight courageously you will not be lost. My maternal love will recompense you for all your tribulations in that terrible night and the morning will dawn magnificently and will calm the fears of that short and terrible night. . . .

The fear of the great and unexpected cataclysm, which will never before have been so extensive down the centuries, will mark the beginning of the Reign of God on Earth.

. . . watch and pray, waiting with faith and in a state of grace the great event. Blessed are those who have believed in my words and suffered in the name of God without need of other revelations.

From Rome, 27 September 1970.

The Earth as We see It

If only Man could see the Earth as we see it, the spectacle which would present itself before his eyes would fill his heart with terror. He would see geysers blowing off evil-smelling material over a large area of Earth: in this way the bad will invade the Earth and will snuff out the delicate flame of good which is trying to rise into the sky. This pestilential condensation will spread over the entire Earth until humanity, a prey because they are undefended against the huge poisonous cloud, is overcome by the increasing growth of the forces of evil. There will be no more flowers or plants of any species but only lichens, fungi and plants without shape; no more animals but only mites, tape-worms and leeches. There will be no death, but the changes of everything into semi-gaseous substances which are the various components of evil.

This ball of compressed energy which will divide the world obtains its energy and will come to an end in an explosion of such size which has never before been seen. This will reduce it to dust which will be spread about the universe.

From Florence, 6 January 1971.

Everything round You already Shakes and Quivers . . .
and Advances

Above all I ask you to be on your guard and not to waste your time in useless lawsuits, not to try and understand what crowds do and not to take part in the stupidities of the moment. I ask you above all for those who are not strong enough and in the midst of a crowd, of a real crowd, could get swept away from them. Remain outside any sort of demonstration, try not to judge it nor to aggravate it, neither with words nor with acts all that trembles and shakes around you.

I tell you that there are seven on this dyke and this abyss, but not seven taking any part. But you are not to turn back. And now, do not bank it up mindlessly but with purpose, as this dyke will save your land again and again, so build up this dyke with every means at your disposal as I have told you, with everyone and everything that you see, as that small piece of stone which seems too small to bother with could be the one to give way and let the dyke slip away to the edge of the precipice.

I have said that you cannot turn back, as to turn back means that the creature has changed his position, is already forgotten and above all has already been destroyed. You cannot turn back as everything around you advances either backwards or forwards and if not in the form of Light.

From Piacenza, 1971.

Progress is in Loving One Another which Unites Men

While history begins at the third millennium, I tell you to embrace yourselves once again in the shadow of the menace which is about to come, because your affection forms a barrier against the evil and which will hold back the tremendous assault.... Love yourselves in the name of Christ and your religious attitude will become perfect. Before the start of the new millennium, human values will be greatly changed and faith will be enriched by contributions by logic and science ... Humanity will move towards great political unions and spiritual ones as well. There will be no new religions, but the existing ones will be brought together in a union of faith which will embrace the whole world. Progress will not be in rivalry which divides people, but in loving one another which unites all men.

From Ali del Pensiero, April 1933.

The end of our Evolutive Cycle

The elements will dissolve but before they come together again the Earth will have something like a separation of its members, and its structure will have to contract and this will be in the form of earthquakes, huge waves and settlements of soil. As a result sky and earth will melt, not to disappear but to change into the form of a semi-transparent globe, on which entities will be of a liquid form; language will not be necessary because thought transference will exist all over the world.

Men will not be inactive and will produce books in fluid material. The various types of living creatures will have wings only. The transformation will be complete as the laws which govern us today will be changed and gravity will disappear.

Everything will be composed of fluid and the dazzle from the celestial vault will have entered successfully; so the stars will be seen in their constellations, seeming to follow man, and the various worlds will be able to communicate with each other. The living world, during this transformation will undergo a violation and a contraction and thus the greatest amount of suffering too, because the strong contrast between the material and astral energy will break itself on this to hasten evolution.

When the evolution slows down, the Eternal Principle will hasten it up again with the vehemence of a cataclysm. That humanity will not have your way of thinking as it will have been completely changed by the pressure of that energy which is called electricity; it is only in this way that men walk and renew their bodies. You only have a pale reflection of the power of x-rays, while the infinite ocean which contains it, tries to lessen all vital movements.

From Milan, 1933.

A Solar Cross will Announce that the End of the World is Near

Humanity is racing towards a renewal, in other words, the world is doing this. It runs towards points which exist already and its trail, which is slightly luminous, remains.

Humanity does not see a limited and forgotten horizon which repels forces which overcome its judgement, if it is not in harmony with Supreme Law. The shadow which thickens up in the vastness of space is multiplied a hundred times because blindness affects the world.

From where comes this mass that is even an outlet for a harmonious and eternal movement? This is the question, the suspense. There are many ways of answering this question. In a favourable way it is said: Advance towards higher evolution, towards a radiant affirmation of faith. . . .

To those who have faith I say: Do not lose your vital spark, take it to warmer centres, as we shall be recalled to the reality which the human being lives in every act. Having the faith does not mean adding to the dogma or pronouncing a new creed, it means bringing to life every single mass of people, and thus, all humanity . . .

Oh, Humanity, you will work to cut thyself off from pain and to prevent anyone else from feeling ill. Look out to feel once more He Who is in the world until the end of Eternity. It will not be a Cross with nails, but a solar Cross shining in Thee, radiating your life all round, a solar Cross which announces coming events to the world.

The Eternal will come to help you. You know how to understand his recall, his admonition, his Love.

From Ali del Pensiero, 1935.

Men Recognize Each Other

. . . and men, become brothers as they were at the beginning of Creation, all recognize each other, all recording their different ages and different modes of dress, becoming one age – the age of brotherhood, and one mode of dress – that of Love.

There is need neither for men to be tormented by their bodies, nor for complicated machines to ensure that they do not hear, and if brothers talk at a distance they will help each other at a distance . . . until the last darkness disappears and the last stages become light.

Blessed are the first to do this! They will be the

humble Masters of all, listened to, loved, blessed. And you will be the first to continue in that faith.

From Alaya, Venice, October 1969.

Humanity of Tomorow

(This message comes from France by means of M. Saltzamanu of Paris, and was reproduced by Ali del Pensiero in Milan, March 1933).

We are on the eve, in the occult world, of extra-ordinary events which will take place on your planet in sensational happenings in every field. The Entity will hasten to add its forces to those men on Earth who wish to re-establish the reign of peace. Man will have to act speedily and well if he wants to avoid the forces of evil which work upon man to hinder the path of progress. The Divine Messengers which will carry the good word to the four corners of the Earth have already reunited. The Annunciation will be renewed and the Earth will beat with hope and love because He who must save the world once more is preparing for his mission.

(And behold once more a vision of the destructive movement which passes in front of the eyes.)

The waves will disappear and the heavy fluids which encircle the Earth will give way little by little under pressure from the white forces. They fight now to hold up their heads against the final spasms of the tempest. Afterwards, from all the paths of Activity by Man, intellectual, moral, spiritual, psychic, will come the saving wave against spiritual crime.

Courage and faith! It is no longer time for hesitation and turning about: Man must quickly understand and rapidly realize the new ways of a new civilization.

The world is at the start of going through gigantic movements ... The last period, in the sphere of politics and social movements, will be named the 'seal' of altruism, thoughtful in activity and rapidity of execu-tion. Those who wish to take command will have to have a sharp intuition and have exemplary wisdom in their decisions. There is no time now to complete projects. It is the action in mass, the sudden penetration of thought, and the speedy understanding by the intelligence of things which are coming. The pioneers must overcome their enthusiasm and enter into the new life! No more indolence, linked with two-faced diplomacy and a strident nationalism and with a feeble political policy. Loyalty, and the direct clean blow, will have to guide the acts of future governors. Do not forget that they will have to raise the world from the most dangerous catastrophe that it has ever known. This is not a matter of the interest of the one or the other, it concerns the life of the whole of Humanity, and those to whom the destinies of the people are entrusted take on a tremendous burden, but if they carry out their tasks well they will be known as Saviours.

(And here is a heroic vision of future days.)

Light and Peace! Soon the torch of spiritual liberation will rise into the cloudy sky. The chains which hold the spirit prisoner in the flesh have gone. God will open to the Spirit a lighted field towards these visible places and will permit the incarnate spirit to acquire once again the celestial spaces. Intuition and direct vision will become part of the inheritance of men on Earth and soon the generations to come will possess these divine gifts as you possess the word and the will. Minds filled with the love of humanity will sacrifice themselves and be born again to help the world. Others, who would have had to remain calm, work up the forces of good; because everyone wants to take part in the spiritual resurrection of humanity tomorrow. Courage! You are coming to the end of the road! Man sees the hand of his God who will help him to reach the highest peak.

There will be a Return to the First Splendour of Faith

... it was easy to sow the tares in the field of good ears of wheat and thus confound ideas, beliefs, rites and traditions. But graver damage will be done to my Church as soon as the astute instigator succeeds in persuading the Heads of my flock to make use of politics, the sword and of fierce storms, in the false fear that otherwise they will not be able to overcome my doctrine.

I tell you that the Redemption will be completed more quickly by Love, in humility and sacrifice and in poverty. Now the great evil will be put right. Now the transformation will cause a return to the original splendour of faith. Then there will be the Reign of my Light.

Thus the New Church, turned to the pureness of its beginnings, will truly have one sole Pastor ...

From Alaya, Venice, October 1969.

'Seven Signs, You will be Recognized once more.'

This affirmation is often repeated. In the order of things nothing happens indiscriminately and this is not something that happens by chance.

Everything that is born, just as everything that dies, is regulated by laws. Nevertheless certain men who tend to regulate everything, strangely believe that one's own most important asset, namely life itself, can depend on chance. It is a sign which everyone bears in himself, a sign invisible to the eyes of men, but very clear to Him who governs life from a higher plane. He creates each one diverse and distinct from everyone else. That sign, which everyone carries in himself, is the sign of his own destiny, made by action that is complete. It is a personal and exclusive light, quite visible and impossible to darken by any other means.

The lack of distinction will be the worst of the injustices. And that will not happen where everyone moves clearly and is governed by laws.

This personal light, which is the spiritual grade of everyone, can be modified. The element most important in making this change is the attitude within to the fact of existence. Those who respond to hate and violence by similar hate and violence put themselves on the same negative plane and are thus subject to all the counter action. They will now be struck down as will also be struck down those who have fear, producing the effect of attracting to themselves that which they fear most.

In this way the attitude of everyone during the crucial period of the calamity, will be the measure by which he is weighed at the end of his own salvation. But the strongest forces of salvation are faith and love. This attitude, apart from being protective, will attract the best type of energy, and bring into action the forces which act positively.

The basis of love and of hate are profoundly different in their nature. Love is naturally creative, including everyone, for the purpose of understanding it, working together in the same sphere, and increases the size of the positive nucleus which exists inside everyone. This love, feeding every part, gives power to the light which is in everyone, although not always in the same way, and is the saviour from destruction.

The action of the other emotion, hate, on the contrary is destructive and decomposing. This hate wants to eliminate and destroy the thing hated.

'Seven signs will be recognized.' The distinctive sign, its own spiritual light, is the hallmark of faith and love which makes it recognizable. This is what the Evangelist means:

'Then shall two be in the field; the one shall be taken, and the other left. Two women shall be grinding at the mill; the one shall be taken, and the other left.' (Matthew 24 : 40–1.) 'Remember Lot's wife. Whosoever shall seek to save his life shall lose it; and whosoever shall lose his life shall preserve it.... there shall be two men in one bed; the one shall be taken, and the other shall be left.' (Luke 17 : 32–4.)

11

THE END OF THE WORLD IN THE GOSPELS AND IN REVELATION

> *And when these things begin to come to pass, then look up, and lift up your heads; for your redemption draweth night.* Luke 21 : 28.

In Biblical prophecy the expression 'time' occurs over and over again. It is found in Ezekiel, in Revelation and in the Gospels. In modern terms we call it an era or a cycle with reference to a phase or a period of history which is part of a larger epoch.

Our age is the end of a great cyclic period of humanity, the end of a Maha-yuga, according to Hindu cosmology. In New Testament writings the end of the world is never spoken about, but the 'end of the present age'. This concept has been expressed by innumerable prophets and seers and is in harmony with the Scriptures of all men.

New Heavens and New Earths

'The face of the Earth will be renewed,' the ancient prophet has written. It has been noted that there are islands risen up as a result of upheavals of the ground caused by volcanic action. In this way the islands of Hawaii and the Aleutian Islands were formed. A tremendous amount of material is brought up from the bed of the sea permeated with water. The opposite happens when land disappears into the sea. The birth and death of entire continents takes place in just the same way in the course of tens of thousands of years. The most recent island is Surtsey, which rose in the

Atlantic in 1963 off the coast of Iceland about 120 kilometres to the south-east of Reykjavik.

'The Time is at Hand.'

Many times in Revelation comes the warning 'The time is at hand.'

'And behold I come quickly; and my reward is with me, to give every man according as his work shall be. I am Alpha and Omega, the beginning and the end, the first and the last. Blessed are they that do his command- ments, that they may have right to the tree of life, and may enter in through the gates into the city. For with- out are dogs, and sorcerers, and whoremongers, and murderers, and idolaters, and whosoever loveth and maketh a lie.' (Revelation 22 : 12–15.) The adamic generation is about to pass away. 'This generation will not pass away before my words will be fulfilled,' said Jesus. The announcement of the New Reign of the Millennium is associated with the second coming of Christ.

On the feast of Christ the King, on 30 October 1967, the following message came to St. Damiano:

'Pray because the Virgin Mother is coming with a great light over the entire world. Then I see, with a New Reign of Peace, greatness, goodness and happiness.'

What will Happen

The picture which the Scripture draws of the end of world is impressive. The Gospels, and even more Revela- tion, describe it in gloomy and dramatic colours.

'This know also, that in the last days perilous times shall come. For men shall be lovers of their own selves, covetous boasters, proud, blasphemers, disobedient to parents, unthankful, unholy. Without natural affection, truce breakers, false accusers, incontinent, fierce, des- pisers of those that are good.' (St. Paul in II Tomothy 3 : 1–3).

Everything is evil in all aspects.

'In the latter times some shall depart from the faith, giving heed to seducing spirits and doctrines of devils; Speaking lies in hypocrisy; having their conscience seared with a hot iron.' (I Timothy 4 : 1–2.) 'Exercise thyself rather unto godliness.' (4 : 7.)

'And ye shall be betrayed both by parents, and brethren, and kinsfolks, and friends; and some of you shall they cause to be put to death.' (Luke 21 : 16.)

And in a crescendo without pause from particular to collective:

'For nation shall rise against nation, and kingdom against kingdom and there shall be famines and pestilences, and earthquakes, in divers places. All these are the beginnings of sorrows.' (Matthew 24 : 7–8.)

Nature itself, indeed, violated by man will rebel. Cataclysms of all types, floods, atmospheric upsets with the resulting great destruction, added to which will be pestilences, famine, wars and massacres by men who will in the last days give way to the most base delinquent actions, scandals, tyranny, homicide. The darkening of conscience always comes before the darkening and extinguishing of actions. That which disturbs man today and throws the minds into confusion are the evident causes of that which seems to get nearer with the inexorability of that which has already been written. And what has written in the invisible as man himself and his own actions.

The awakening of many volcanoes will add to the growing impression of disaster. One can almost hear the voice of the Book of Revelation: 'Woe, woe...'

'Immense earthquakes will profoundly disturb the Earth's crust, burying' (as in the days of Lemuria and Atlantis) 'nations and kingdoms according to the areas of the continents submerged.'

Lands and countries would disappear and the actual distribution of seas would be changed by the works of successive cataclysms. According to some commentators, Germany, Russia and the Balkans would become seas.

146

G. Barberin says that 'the southern part of France would be submerged under the waters as would also be the greater part of the Italian peninsula, Rome included. Spain would remain almost untouched. Japan would be almost removed from the map.'

But how is this known with such exactness? They even pretend to know just how the future map of the world will be drawn. It seems that some of the specialists in oceanography have already noticed upheavals and convulsions in the depths of the sea and found shallows there which have not appeared beforehand on maps.

The Signs of the Coming End

Is the end of the world coming now?

In 1360 St. Brigid said 'The world is nearing its final epoch which is dawning now, and which will last until the day of judgement.'

In the Gospel it is written: '... this gospel of the kingdom shall be preached in all the world for a witness unto all nations; and then shall the end come.' (Matthew 24 : 14.) Christianity is a universal religion and not local as Judaism, Buddhism or Islam. Therefore it must be known by everyone before the end of the epoch which can be said to belong to it.

The end of the world is also predicted in St. Luke's Gospel, (21 : 24) 'And they shall fall by the edge of the sword, and shall be led away captive into all nations: and Jerusalem shall be trodden down of the Gentiles, until the times of the Gentiles be fulfilled.'

By the name of Gentiles (a word deriving from *gentes*, nations), the Scriptures indicate the idolatrous countries and all those who did not belong to the Jewish nation. They are pagans or enemies. Christian brotherhood had not yet been established. St. Paul is called the Apostle of the peoples because he was especially interested in the conversion of the pagans to Christianity.

It is appropriate to this time to think of the reconstruction of the Kingdom of Israel as a sovereign and independent state after the huge disaster of genocide which has no equal in Teutonic barbarism, and then from the bloody struggles with the neighbouring Arab peoples: the forced dispersion of its sons has come to an end as they can freely return to the ancient fatherland without restriction. The two-thousand year cycle of prophetic condemnation verified in a tremendous way in this manner, has come to an end for good. Therefore with this the time of the Gentiles has also been fulfilled which was clearly foretold by the words of Christ. By these prophecies we can see that we are already entering the time when all things will be brought to an end.

There are three signs that the end of time is at hand. (1) The universal forecast of the Gospels. (2) The end of the time of the Gentiles with the return of the Hebrews to their own land. (3) 'The abomination of desolation positioned in a sacred place.'

Is the Time of the Gentiles indeed Over?

The Hebrew state has been reconstituted, but Jerusalem, as a result of the fighting going on with the Arabs, seems to be still trampled underfoot by the Gentiles, for that reason, according to some, the time does not seem to be fulfilled for everyone. We have to await a permanent peace to see if we are truly at the end of the world.

The time of the Gentiles or the Nations, of which they speak, is a historical period which comprises the centuries which the prophet Daniel indicates with the expression 'the holy people will come into their power for a time, and then for two and a half times. Then at last the judgement will come: the power will be taken away from those people, and it will be destroyed and annihilated for ever.'

Those students who play around with calculating dates and times say that the three and a half times of Daniel are made up of 1,260 years, a 'time' being worked out at 360 years. But the time of the Gentiles means seven 'times' or ages. In the Biblical book of Leviticus there is a statement that Israel must be punished at the end of seven ages, that is 360 × 7 or 2,520 years. The age in which we live is the seventh and last, which is the time of the end.

From when must we begin to count? Once more we must go to the dates. But in prophecy, as we have pointed out over and over again, we must beware of expecting an event to occur exactly when forecast, as when given in more detail than the year it has a value solely to the man who wishes to use it as a point of reference.

The Abomination of Desolation

The abomination is the attempt on the part of Man to sit like God in the temple and the presumptuous attempt to climb the stairway to Olympus, it is titanism, the deification of tiny I, the puerile insanity of Man who is unable to measure his own wretchedness, unable to realize the true state of man and to perceive the divine largeness. The man of the twentieth century flies in Space and uses automation. His scientists do not know how to understand the limitations of man and believe that he can do everything, and that there is nothing at all greater than he is. Pride and presumption make man blind, and the blind man does not know where to place his feet and how to avoid walking into obstacles.

'When ye therefore shall see the abomination of desolation, spoken of by Daniel the prophet, stand in the holy place, (whoso readeth, let him understand:) Then let them which be in Judea flee into the mountains: Let him which is on the housetop not come down to take any thing out of his house: Neither let him which is in the field return to take his clothes. And woe unto them that are with child, and to them that give suck in those days!' (Matthew 24 : 15–19.)

'But pray ye that your flight be not in the winter, neither on the sabbath day: For then shall be great tribulation, such as was not since the beginning of the world to this time, no, nor ever shall be, And except those days should be shortened, there should no flesh be saved: but for the elect's sake those days shall be shortened.' (Matthew 24 : 20-2.)

The abomination of desolation, about which we have written in Chapter 6, is, above all, the state of complete internal emptiness, to which the minds have been reduced who have believed in the doctrines of atheism and materialism. In the minds of men, which should be a temple of God, the most complete desolation will reign. This will refer also to those who have turned from the faith when they should have been its chief upholders.

False Prophets and False Christs

There are innumerable cases of directions given from God to guide the human race.

But, among these others can be found who are not in the least altruistic, but think only of personal vanity, their own interests, having power in their hands or their own pleasure. Outwardly they seem helpful and motivated by altruism, otherwise they are not accepted. They are the false prophets and false Christs against whom we have to be on guard. Not only from people, but from ideas and banners as well.

Jesus has said 'For there shall arise false Christs, and false prophets, and shall show great signs and wonders; insomuch that, if it were possible, they shall deceive the very elect.' (Matthew 24 : 22.)

The end of the world with its confusion, sadness and hopes, is very suitable to the verbal wanderings of these deceivers. The chosen will not be deceived. The deceiver will have measured the gullibility of men and will know the elect and the reprobate. Those who let themselves be taken in sink down to the level of the deceiver. Those who fall into his net are deprived of the ability to judge for themselves and are also attracted by egoistic forces which point out their own personal advantage.

Among the false prophets of the end of the world, the

Marxist ideology is one of those who promised happiness on Earth, basing it on material happiness, but without giving what it promises. It is the more deceptive because not only does it not fulfil its promises on the material sphere but it does not give any happiness at all, being a wretchedly shoddy imitation of Christianity. People who are immature have not realized this fact.

The false Christs and the pseudo saviours from injustice are not genuine as their standards are those of the Earth and do not carry people to higher planes. As with some ministers of religion, priests, pastors and political and social benefactors, they seek a proselitism of partial salvation and do not seek to redeem the whole man, bringing him up from animal level.

There are false Christs and false prophets who pretend to fix the whole man in the things of the Earth or the depths of the subconscous, and ignore the higher things: pseudo scientists and preachers of ideas which they claim to be scientific, but which have no place in the divine plan, and hold back Man to the confines of the Earth.

The prodigies which are recognized by science are not certain to end on the higher planes. Those who confuse others can be considered as false prophets, but only on the level of phenomena which are momentary and illusory. Apart from these areas, this science is not able to go as it does not know how. Indeed, this only goes to demonstrate even more strongly that it is the life of the spirit in everyone that gives them life.

It is enough to think about the really saintly prodigies, and about the sages and the yogi who move on a much higher plane, and to think on the laws which govern the life on the invisible plain. The prodigies of science dazzle the weak and prevent them from making progress, they snare and hold them up and do not inspire them, making them think that science is in everything.

The person who is most important in Christian prophecy, the outstanding figure in the present cycle is known as Christ, and His second coming will bring this era to an end.

Before we can understand Antichrist we must first refer to Christ Himself, in opposition to Whom stands Antichrist.

Christ is the Power for the good, the Fountain of Love, the Source of the Great Light, Who is capable of redeeming and saving Man. He who is not in harmony with Him is against Him.

Human life is inextricably bound to fighting, not necessarily one against the other, but between internal forces that exist in everyone. The others are only false objectives and sometimes pretexts for forces working within a man. The conflict goes on in every man to the end of his life and ends with the defeat of the negative forces, the antichrist which is in everyone. Thus everyone is a battlefield. Those who still have something of the bestial in them, primordial instincts, pride, egotism, hate, sensuality, disappear little by little with the advance of the light of the good, just as the shade disappears in front of the sun.

The negative forces of the bad, opposed to Christ, with their hundred names and their thousand aspects, arrogance, thirst for dominance, intolerance, violence, are impersonated by Antichrist, the real evil, the manifest emissary of Satan (II Thessalonians 2 : 9), whose successors are deceptive and limited in power. Indeed in the Book of Job it is written : 'Satan hurts only if God allows him to.'

A Person? Collectivism? Idealogy?

The atheist, materialist and pagan society is the most manifest expression of Antichrist. Jesus in the Gospel had already warned that many would be drawn away to mistaken ideologies with a flattering appearance. Marxism in all its versions boasts these characteristics of which the most important is the counterfeiting of Christianity.

The beast which comes from the sea in the Book of Revelation, has been identified by many with this force working for separation, whose beliefs and cult of hate and violence are in opposition to love. Origen, Lattanzio and St. Augustine have recognized Antichrist as a collective human force, a current philosophy, an antichristian ideology.

According to St. Paul, Antichrist, by virtue of Satan, is the person who will bring about the final decay of faith. The political and doctrinal antichrist, symbolized by the two beasts of the apocalypse, is a creature of Evil.

Today, crowds of people who are sceptical and indifferent to sane and constructive ideas, run after the will o' the wisp which has been ingeniously made to resemble the truth and which has been placed before them.

Antichrists, not one but many are not only forces, tendencies and ideologies which are destructive and movements of hate and violence, but they are also people who draw this negativity to them and express it. Revolts, wars and ruin are the logical consequences of their actions in the heart of all men and then the whole world.

The personal Antichrists

Antichrist is a prophetic reality. Every idea takes its place in an individual's mind, and men impersonate ideology. They can do this because of personal and disintegrating Antichrists, professional spreaders of hate, violence and war.

St. Paul says that the presence of many Antichrists will be one of the signs that the end is drawing near.

In a true sense all are Antichrists who teach and practise doctrines and theories opposite to the teaching of Christ.

Peculiar to the Hebrew people, chosen for this task, the destructive and anti-christian forces of the last days rise up in opposition to the great light of Christ. Everything which today causes desecration is the clear expression of this complex of dark forces in movement which acts in the individual (Freud's theory) and in society as a whole (Marx's theory).

The figure of Antichrist which blossomed out in leaps and bounds from time to time in the history of man, assumes forms and virulence clearer than ever in this final period and his actions are especially subtle and cunning.

In the *Protocolli* of Savi Anziani of Sion, the distant Hebrew origin of Antichrist is pointed out and it also declares that 'war and the class struggle will destroy the Christian people'.

Their Dreary Influence

It is natural that in the Christian Era everything is fixed on the great light of Christ and, as a result, people guard against the shade which follows in contrast to the light.

Christ is light, love and truth and expresses this in unity, completion and perfection. Antichrist is the negative figure, the shade. In him is seen the action of Christ turned upside down.

Just as with a monkey, Antichrist mimics the appearance of the person he wishes to imitate in order to deceive while his teachings are substantially the opposite, that is darkness, hate, evil, division, disintegration and thus confusion and regression.

Antichrist has his forerunner in the Biblical serpent, who came before the seducer of the world of Revelation, also born as a definite person. In the various epochs of human history he has come from time to time in people who have earned a notoriety with their destructive and evil actions.

Disregarding those Antichrists who have gone before, we find ourselves today under the evil influence of Antichrist in an ever-growing crescendo which consists today of the materialism and atheism which have invaded every field and every human activity in the attempt to root up humanity, to break down society and isolate men.

His main object is to remove the idea of God and every religious feeling. Of his followers Marx and Freud are among the most active personification of these dissolving and negative forces which prepare for the epoch of chaos. The first increase in this chaos took place in 1966. From this year onwards indeed, in the life of so many men, there has been a remarkable change towards the final epoch. The anarchic sexual orgy that is disrupting mankind at the present time and the confusion in ideas and teachings are reaching to the culmination of human folly, in debauchery, revolt, disorder which will speed up in 1972 and even more in 1975.

Already many people can no longer distinguish the good from the evil, the right from the wrong, the just from the unjust, the true from the false, putting everything on the same level.

Everyone wants to obtain things and not to give things. Egotism whets the appetite with the thirst for pleasure. Possession and domination inducing convulsive action. Even speaking the same language, as in the tower of Babel people neither understand nor feel for each other.

This epoch of chaos, according to certain commentators of Nostradamus, will last six years and will give way to a period of growing disorder by the coming of the Seventh Antichrist. Men will be demolishing what have been the basic fundamentals of civilization, without succeeding to find yet the secure bases for a new building. Indeed the demolition men are not capable of reconstruction. Their arms, hate and violence, tyrannical force and tax collecting are no use at all in construction but only give rise to more evil. Only love can build.

The Seventh Antichrist, according to Nostradamus,

will come from Islam. His principal aim, the diffusion of antichristian ideas, just as those who came before him, sizzling with hate, revolt and materialism, worse than ever before. His influence and power will extend even to Africa.

The Last Antichrist

The last Antichrist will have in him all the evil and all the characteristics of his predecessors and from whom come all the violently destructive powers: Pride, riches, government, dishonesty. According to an old Hebrew tradition he will be a Jew from the tribe of Dan. He will know all languages. 'He will seduce with masked violence and flattery,' says Salvaneschi, 'and will have as servants, pleasures, money, sensuality, illusions and vices.'

He will live as an unknown man until his appearance. Nostradamus says that his struggle will last twenty-seven years. According to the seer of Salon, the history of the world will come to an end with the Eighth Antichrist: the Asiatic. Today because we live in the age before the apocalypse, we can unfortunately breathe the atmosphere. This is just because no prophetic test can learn the number of Antichrist. Many commentators think the end is coming and is that which corresponds to the number 666 and closes that period known as the sign of the Fishes.

Are We in the Age of the Beast?

There are not a few who remember that Satan will truly awaken from his lethargy. It is enough to look around to see how much society and the men of today are different from what they were a few years ago: a change in every field and not only speedy but always for the worse towards the confused worship of the machine.

Liberty, having become licence, expresses itself in the abolition of every brake and the rejection of all external authority without having replaced it by self-discipline; in dominating others; in personal profit; in sex carried on at a level below that of animals.

Deceit and intrigue seem to have become almost normal in the attainment of the bounds of egotism. He who should obey gives the orders and the man who should be learning arrogantly pretends to teach.

The unleashing of huge appetites in those who should be educated are the frequent works of unscrupulous men who rekindle the base instincts in others for their own greedy ends.

The cult of pleasure, money and possession is evident manifestation of the cult of the beast; and tempts man in every age, but it has never been so widespread as it is now.

Human laws which should at least limit this exist, which only reflects the lowering of general standards in morals and fashion. A weak ruling class, representing people of little moral evolution in a corrupt democracy, base their actions on those of demagogues.

The Acts of the Evil One

The manifestations of Antichrist conform to the programme of this evil personage. Because his ability is to deceive, mimicking the works of Christ, he will draw to him a number of disciples who will eagerly accept the doctrines which he teaches. In the Second Epistle to the Thessalonians, St. Paul writes of his acts in anticipation:

'... son of perdition; Who opposeth and exalteth himself above all this is called God or that is worshipped; so that he as God sitteth in the Temple of God, showing himself that he is God.' (2 : 3, 4.) And later: 'Even him, whose coming is after the working of Satan with all power and signs and lying wonders, and with all deceivableness of unrighteousness in them that perish; because they received not the love of the truth, that they might be saved. And for this cause God shall send them strong delusion, that they should believe a lie.' (2 : 9–11.)

He goes on to say that his works will at first be secret but later he will act openly with all his arms. After a brief triumph he will be vanquished by Christ. The same concept is in the mind of St. John when he announces the defeat of the enemies of God in the Book of Revelation.

In the prophecy of Orval it is said that 'the man of evil will be born of mixed blood and will carry out infamies of all kinds.' Other prophecies announce too that a great persecution will take place, greater than has ever been seen ... the years will be shortened like months, the months like weeks and the weeks like days and the days like hours ... During the reign of Antichrist, according to the prophecy attributed to Sibilla Tiburtina, two illustrious men will appear, who will announce the coming of the Lord. Antichrist will kill him, and two days afterwards the Lord will rise again ...

It is he who confirms that the Antichrist is the key to understanding the *Centuries* of Nostradamus. Indeed the Seer has a lot to say about him:

'The child' (Antichrist) 'born of a monk and a nun who abandoned him so that he would die of hunger, will be close to him who crawls' (the serpent)...

'He will never weary of confusing the great liar...

'His bloody war will last 27 years, and whoever is not of his opinion will be killed, imprisoned or exiled. Blood will flow and the ground will be covered with bodies and the water will become red and discolour the hailstones...'

Sibilla Tiburtina thinks that Antichrist will come from the tribe of Dan and will die on the Mount of Olives at Jerusalem under the blows of the Archangel Michael (Perhaps on Good Friday 1999 – that is 2 April 1999), the Great Justiciary, who will bring him down and will banish him to the nether regions. The reign of Antichrist will last for three years. He will feign a resurrection and an ascension in order to mimic Christ. But at the end he will be struck down by a flash of lightning.

The Epoch of the Final Antichrist

We are somewhat flattered to be the contemporaries
of Antichrist and not even cheered too much by recognizing his evil acts. The prophets of the Christian
inspiration are almost all in agreement that in the last
days the serpent, the tempter, the enemy and the seducer
will reappear.

St. Hildegarde, abbess of the Benedictines of Rupertsberg on the Rhine who lived from 1098 to 1170, wrote:
'The son of perdition who will reign for a very short
time, will appear in the last days.'

Anna Katherine Emmerich (1774–1824) in her ecstasies
used to speak in Aramaic, the language spoken by Jesus;
she had the stigmata. She affirmed that this is the pre-
apocalyptic epoch.... Before 2000 Lucifer would be set
free for a certain time. 'Certain demons will have to be
set at liberty first, for the correction and temptation of
men. I think in our days he will not be unleashed, but
others think he will be unleashed a little after our days.'

Wladimir Soloviev, the great spiritualist, the disciple
of Dostoievsky, placed the birth of Antichrist in 1954.

Pius X in his encyclical of 4 October 1903 affirmed that
'the son of perdition of whom the Apostle spoke' was
already in the world. But at the second coming of Christ
the Evil one will disappear as the shade at the advance of
the Sun.

The Return of Christ

The events which will shake the Earth, will culminate
in the second coming of Christ, which will be the manifestation of the greatest spiritual force which will descend on Man. In the history of Man it is pointed out that
when the spiritual life is low and the moral standards
are going down, the Person sent by God appears to bring
Men back to the road they have abandoned. This is
affirmed explicitly in the Bhagavad-gîtâ (IV, 7–8):
'Every time that the law becomes ineffective and

licence increases I shall appear. In order to save the good people and to destroy the evil ones and to restore the Law to its full power I shall be born from time to time.'

Ater the death of Jesus, the most faithful declare that He will return. He Himself has promised to return, but it is not certain if the disciples did not imagine this. Matthew, Mark and Luke speak of the return of Christ, and it is also mentioned in Revelation.

In the Second Epistle to the Thessalonians St. Paul warns against belief in the immediate return of Our Lord: 'Let no man deceive you by any means: for that day shall not come, except there come a falling away first, and that man of sin be revealed, the son of perdition.' (II Thessalonians, 2 : 3.)

Jesus said '. . . Take heed that no man deceive you. For many shall come in my name saying, I am Christ; and shall deceive many. And ye shall hear of wars and rumours of wars; see that ye be not troubled; for all these things must come to pass, but the end is not yet.' (Matthew 24 : 4–6.) 'All these are the beginnings of sorrows.' (Matthew 24 : 8.)

In adversity man shows his strength or his weakness. Many will renounce their own faith, showing themselves in their true light.

When Christ Returns

St. Paul confirms that no one knows the time when the Saviour will return. The expectation must be postponed again and again. Indeed in the first century everyone awaited what they called the *parousia*, the presence, the apparition, or the manifestation of the Saviour. Everyone wanted to see the return of Jesus before they died. It was a long wait, which went on from century to century, people lost hope, renewed it, and never lost it down the centuries.

The error was in the mistaken idea on the significance of the return of Christ. We all know who started this mistake. St. Paul wrote to the Christians at Thessalonika to reassure them that the return of Christ was not imminent, but he wrote as if both he and his hearers would take part in it.

It is natural that people wanted to know when all these events would happen which had been predicted. But Jesus said that the hour was known only to the Father. He went on to say that the Lord would come unexpectedly 'Like a thief in the night.' (Matthew 24 : 43—Luke 12 : 39.)

He spoke like this, certainly, so that people would always be ready for the great event. Had he given them the exact date people would have given themselves over to a good time especially if it were a long time ahead, and postponed their salvation until a short while before the return was expected.

The Advance Signs of the Second Coming of Christ

The second coming of Christ will coincide with the end of the present Christian era. It has already been said that this will be preceded by great calamities. In his day St. Paul wished to indicate the events that would have to take place first. In order to convince his hearers better he pointed out the signs which would have to precede the second coming of Christ. They are: (1) the general loss of faith together with the dominance of the flesh over the spirit; (2) the appearance of Antichrist, the son of Perdition (see II Thessalonians 2 : 3).

'... Nevertheless when the Son of Man cometh, can he find faith on the earth?' (Luke 18 : part of v8.) 'And because iniquity shall abound, the love of many shall wax cold.' (Matthew 24 : 12.)

To this will be added what we have already pointed out will mark the end of time, that is, the appearance on earth of Enoch and Elijah, the preaching of the Gospel in all the world, the conversion of the Jews, atmospheric phenomena, and earthquakes, when fire will fall on the Earth. The coming of Christ seems to be that last scene of the great drama which is coming to an end after which ignorant men, smothered with the pleasures of material life, will give themselves over to the sins of before the flood and to sodomy.

'And as it was in the days of Noe, so shall it be also in the days of the Son of man. They did eat, they drank, they married wives and were given in marriage, until the day that Noe entered into the ark, and the flood came and destroyed them all. Likewise also as it was in the days of Lot; they did eat, they drank, they bought, they sold, they planted, they builded; But the same day that Lot went out of Sodom it rained fire and brimstone from heaven, and destroyed them all. Even thus shall it be in the day when the Son of Man is revealed.' (Luke 17 : 26–30.)

When the Day of the Lord will Come

The second coming of Christ is an event of great importance and which attracts universal attention, because it is linked up with the achievement of the Millennium by Man. The prophecies will be realized and unbelievable happenings will be seen. The eyes of men will finally be opened and the mind will understand.

The comings of Christ are in actual fact two, one in humility and the other in Glory. The first has the more truth and which will enter the hearts of those who understand love. It is a light which can illuminate everything and make people see things in another light. This coming will bring light and warmth, the conditions for growing to real truth. The joy of the disciples is expressed in the simple words of Paul: 'And thus we shall be always with the Lord.' But the desire and the waiting will make the time seem longer. At the same time St. Paul wrote: 'We ardently desire to be dissolved and to live with Christ.'

But, for those who look for the Coming in glory, it has been said:

'Immediately after the tribulation of those days shall the sun be darkened, and the moon shall not give her light, and the stars shall fall from heaven, and the powers of the heaven shall be shaken:' (Matthew 24 : 29.)

They are the tremendous phenomena which will come before the manifestation of the Son of Man. Have they a literal or figurative sense? Eclipses of the sun or of values? Of men or of things? Alone they would be absurd. The Gospel of St. Luke gives more detail:

'And there shall be signs in the sun, and in the moon, and in the stars; and upon Earth distress of nations with perplexity; the sea and the waves roaring; Men's hearts failing them for fear, and for looking after those things which are coming on the earth: for the power of heaven shall be shaken. And then shall they see the Son of Man coming in a cloud with power and great glory. And when these things begin to come to pass, then look up and lift up your heads; for your redemption draweth nigh.... And take heed to yourselves, lest at any time your hearts be overcharged with surfeiting, and drunkenness, and cares of this life, and so that day come upon you unawares. For as a snare shall it come on all them that dwell on the face of the whole earth. Watch ye therefore, and pray always, that ye may be accounted worthy to escape all these things that shall come to pass, and to stand before the Son of Man.' (Luke 21 : 25–8, 34–6.) 'And then shall they see the Son of Man coming in the clouds with great power and glory. And then shall he send his angels, and shall gather together his elect from the four winds, from the uttermost part of the earth to the uttermost part of heaven.' (Mark 13 : 26–7.)

St. Paul, too, describes the Parousia, the day of the manifestation of the Lord Jesus together with the angels in power, in the sky in flames and fire.

'For the Lord himself shall descend from heaven with a shout, with the voice of an archangel, and with the trump of God: and the dead in Christ shall rise first: Then we which are alive and remain shall be caught up together with them in the clouds, to meet the Lord in the air: and so shall we ever be with the Lord.' (I Thessalonians 4 : 16–17).

And note that he insists on the fact of Jesus coming on the clouds.

'For when they say, Peace and safety; then sudden destruction cometh upon them, as travail upon a woman with child; and they shall not escape.' (I Thessalonians 5 : 3). Thus speaks St. Paul and he goes on '. . . and I pray God your whole spirit and soul and body be preserved blameless unto the coming of our Lord Jesus Christ.' (I Thessalonians 5:23).

'Behold, he cometh with clouds; and every eye shall see him, and they also which pierced him; and all kindreds of the earth shall wail because of him. (Revelation 1 : 7).

Regarding the coming of the Angels with Christ, most prophets interpret this as the physical arrival of inhabitants of other planets at the same time as the spiritual manifestation of the great Light of Christ. These beings, who have evolved far beyond human beings represent the spiritual quality of highness so that they can aid and elevate the spiritual level of the Earth.

The Reign of God

The first Christians hoped that Jesus would return to reign at Jerusalem over the Hebrews or certainly over the whole world as temporal king. They even had discussions on how the power was to be divided up! Only later on did the concept begin to enter peoples' minds that the real kingdom was in heaven, although Christ had warned them repeatedly that 'My kingdom is not of this world.' The power and the glory imagined by materialistic man was human, made of splendour and authority. But the concept held by the evangelists of the reign of God on Earth is very different from the dreams of men who still had a materialistic mentality.

The Vision of the Revelation

The title of the book of Revelation (Apocalypse in Greek and Italian) comes from the first Greek words of the text which does not occur again in the whole book. It means 'Revelation of a hidden truth' with the eschatological sense (from *eschatos*, last) or concerning the last days. The interest in Revelation has always remained alive, and even today, despite the widespread scepticism, arouses the curiosity and attention of many people. The symbolic vision, of profound suggestive power, also in its extreme drama, with obscure touches of tragedy, is not a message of terror, but of comfort and the certainty of the final triumph of the Lamb over the beast. This, in other respects, is the meaning of the prophecies. They do not aim to cause fear, but to stir into action the sleepy, the apathetic, the ignorant, and to strike at the guilty, because they can see the result of the action that they are still determined to do. 'They frighten the wicked' has been written; the others not only have reason to fear but can themselves feel comforted by the path they have chosen, and still feel the joy of goodness that flourishes inside them just as the sower sees the seed sprouting which he has planted out.

At the beginning of the fourth chapter Revelation predicts the events which will take place until the end of the world. In colourful, symbolic and allegoric language, fitting for its Oriental style, it describes calamities, persecutions, loss of belief, and the last judgement.

The struggle between the bad and the good is between the salient points of both. He affirms that the forces of evil will not win and that man will not repent until the very last hour, when the glory of the Lamb will be announced to all who wait for Him.

The Seven Seals and the Horsemen of the Revelation

If it is true that the world will not come to an end with the events which are about to happen, but that they mean only the change to a New Age, it is also true – according to the prophecies – that for those who do not understand the Light it will be as if everything were finished.

The test for the selection of men will be hard, but the number of those who will come through will be great.

To the symbolic visions of the Seers there first appears a white horse and in the saddle a horseman armed with a bow, come to bring peace to men. He is Christ, the divine Archer, who with the bow will strike at the bad, and will convert the whole world with His love: he will open the first seal.

Let us follow the other visions and the breaking of the seven seals.

For the second, behold a red horse and the rider had a great sword in his hand. It is the beginning of war 'and power was given to him that sat thereon to take peace from the earth, and they should kill one another, and there was given to him a great sword.' The class war seems to have been prophesied. The sword is a symbol of military power. The struggle will not be between individual people but collective, between peoples.

At the third seal a black horse appears and the rider has a scales. A voice cries out: 'A measure of wheat for a penny, and three measures of barley for a penny; and see thou hurt not the oil and wine.' Men will lose their faith, but will not lack divine grace (symbolized by the wine and oil). A period of darkness (the black horse). The balance is the symbol of justice: 'You have been weighed in the balance and found wanting.'

The fourth horse was pale and had Death as a rider. The power of Death is to kill by illness and by hunger. The pale colour is that of deceit which carries death with it. Even after the coming of Christ the struggle against evil has not come to an end. There are periods of darkness and famine in the spiritual grace such as atheism, scepticism, enemies to weaken to have once more the joy of faith. The deceiver for those who accept him, bring death. This period will last until the fifth seal is broken.

At the breaking of the fifth seal John saw the Spirits of the Martyrs at the foot of the Altar of God who were singing the praises of God and calling on Justice so that their sacrifice would not be in vain and Humanity could receive the light which marked the end of deception which is worse than the absence of faith.

'He who does not succeed in feeling God' (the atheist) 'is helped by God, but he who accepts the deceiver and offers his services to him and gives him his faith, renounces divine aid.' Thus the prophetically inspired message explains this part of Revelation which we have related. And he adds: 'Be ready, at the attack. I who from the height of my tower can make out clearly the pale horse of the deceiver give the alarm signal as it is my duty. God concedes it to make people hear and understand for His glory.'

The Last Seals are Opened

Evil with its apparent dazzle of false virtue, power and brilliant capacity, draws off many in error. Faith in an idea which does not show its reality to everyone, will be the cause of discord, perplexity and division among men. There will be struggles and collective wars for the faith until the date of the opening of the sixth seal is given. At the opening of this one Revelation speaks of convulsions on Earth, of displacement of islands and siderial revolutions. Coinciding with the opening of the sixth seal is the age of disgrace, the reign of Satan. The cataclysm of fire, which is mentioned in Deuteronomy, will cause the destruction of a continent like Atlantis which was submerged under the waters. Every imaginable cataclysm is less fearful than that which will be seen by the creatures of the earth and also of the astral regions.

This is the famous universal justice! Good and evil.

The terror of the things that happened before that caused all men to invoke God.

'And they said to the mountains and the rocks, Fall on us and hide us from the face of him that sitteth on the throne, and from the wrath of the Lamb: For the great day of his wrath is come; and who shall be able to stand?' (Revelation 6 : 16–17).

But four angels posted at the four positions of the compass symbolizing the Cross, will guard the Earth, ready for the orders of the Lord of the Universe. The Archangel Gabriel will warn:

'Hurt not the earth, neither the sea, nor the trees till we have sealed the servants of God in their foreheads.' (Revelation 7 : 3).

It is a luminous signal, but not of ordinary material.

The signal which will distinguish men in that supreme moment is not a visible sign to the eyes, but it is a signal which gives light to the spirit: intuition. It is a divine gift for those who are ready to receive it. It will be ignored by those who live subject to the limitations of the astral sphere.

The number of saved ones is a great multitude of people of all nations and languages, wearing white stoles and bearing palms in their hands ...

They are those who have purified their spirit so as to deserve the first prize given to those faithful to God. Their number will be greater than those carried away by deception.

Then all, Angels, Elders (symbol of the older fathers who kept their faith) together with the animals (symbol of all the forces of the Universe, of creatures not conscious but who however vibrate with the life of the Universe) in a good spectacle of love, intone their song of adoration and thanks.

The four angels, guardians of the four winds 'because they do not blow', are guarding the things which can carry destruction. The symbolical seal with which the Angels marked the front of men is made of light, like the light of intuition which is the highest means of contact with the higher world.

At the breaking of the Seventh seal there was a

silence weighing on creation, a mysterious pause in which Humanity seemed to have found peace for a moment. It is the moment to hear the voices of silence and to hear what they had to say.

'And I saw the seven angels which stood before God; and to them were given seven trumpets.' (Revelation 8 : 2.)

The prophetic and inspired communication to which we have subjected the foregoing comment goes on like this :

'You understand : every Angel in charge of a ray will have orders to sound the retreat; thus every one of the seven Angels which the virtues of the Infinite possess which appear on the Earth and on the astral plane, will use his influence to illuminate the faithful who are found under his protection, and thus will be made in various ways, with miracles, with visions, with prophecies, given to take the middle road and to accept from God those means of communication between Heaven and Earth. Many, a great many more than now, will help Humanity. It is easy to understand why, it will be to win the battle and to show everyone the final victory of the Good, the triumph of God. Indeed the Angel who, in front of the Altar with a thurible of gold, sends the smoke of the incense to the throne of God, represents the cleverest and most active helpers for whom he looks on Earth. The perfume of incense is the spiritual perfume of elect minds. In the symbol therefore, of the Virgin, after having offered to God the love of the most elect creatures by the fire of the altar (that is love itself), it will return to Earth. Love as you already know, spreads warmth throughout the Universe. Love, sent back on Earth in a very special manner, moves with the planet in a similar manner to the transition of God-Man, and if there are thunders and earthquakes on Earth, with the terror from which those things come.

'Do not marvel, you who read. Love must take an increase of grace and this always comes up after a sin which limits the spirit to become bent down and to understand its own origin. It is planned that the pain becomes ecstasy and joy for those who have grace with them. Every cataclysm brings pain to those who still have to work to purify their spirits and so bring spiritual joy to themselves, and brings spiritual joy to those who already have the white stole which is connected with purification.' (M.G.V. from Ali del Pensiero, June 1933.)

12

THE SECRET OF FATIMA

While the First World War was raging, on 13 May 1917, in Fatima, a small Portuguese village, an extraordinary event took place which will forever remain famous all over the world. To three children, Lucia Do Santos (10 years old) and to her little brother and sister, Jacinta (7 years old) and Francesco Marto (9 years old), carrying a strong light, a very beautiful lady, shining like the sun appeared above a beech tree. She suggested that they pray to bring an end to the war and bring peace on the world. She showed her sadness for the bad which men do and announced the calamities which have struck humanity in this appalling century. The apparitions were repeated. The stimulus of seeing one's errors was characteristic of the message of Fatima.

For those who can understand it, it is to bring out a singular fact, partly to mark the three grades of mystic initiation at Fatima : Francesco saw the Virgin, Giacinta saw her and perceived her, Lucia saw her, perceived her and spoke with her.

The Third Apparition

The most important was the third appearance, 13 July 1917. The Madonna announced the great prophetic event, called the Secret of Fatima. She said that from Russia an evil destiny would come designed to corrupt the people and hurl the nations one against the other, and announced the Second World War.

In 1942, on the twenty-fifth anniversary of the appearances, Pope Pius XII revealed the prophecy through the mouth of Cardinal Schuster. But part of it was concealed, that part which was, naturally, an object of discussion, suspicion, and inference of all types. The part published with ecclesiastical approval is as follows:

'If you do what I tell you, many souls will be saved and we shall have peace. The war is coming to an end; but it does not cease to offend the Lord, and another, more terrible one will break out. When you see a night lit up by an unknown light, you will know that it is the great sign that God gives you of the next punishment of the sins of the world with war, famine and persecution against the Church and against the Holy Father.

'In order to prevent this, I have come to intercede for the consecration of Russia to my Immaculate Heart and the communion of the first sabbaths.

'If you carry out my demands, Russia will be converted and there will be peace. Otherwise the errors (Marxism) will be spread around the world, provoking war and persecution against the Church; many good people will become martyrs, the Holy Father will suffer much; many nations will be suppressed ...' (Here is a secret section which has not yet been revealed). 'But in the end my Immaculate Heart will triumph, the Holy Father will consecrate Russia for me, which will be converted and the world will be granted a period of peace ...'

It is understandable language indicating from what and against what we turn. The strange splendour announced as 'the great sign that God gives you of the next punishment of the sins of the world with war,' came to pass on the night of 25 January 1938, and the press gave full accounts of it the next day. (I have vivid memories of this – translator.)

The Second World War broke out and we all know the consequences all over the Earth.

The Secret that was not Revealed

What does this secret consist of? Why is it more useful not to reveal it?

This mysterious and controversial part of the message

172

of Fatima was held for a long time in the bishopric in Leiria. Everyone awaited its publication when the message, taken to the Vatican, was opened. But the waiting was in vain as nothing was said officially. One new fact, however, came into the politics of the Holy See; the preoccupation more than ever with the starting of a dialogue with Russia. Indeed, contrary to the tradition of slow and cautious transformation of every position taken up, was the unexpected turn in policy of the previous Pope, Pius XII. From the knowledge that this research had taken place and how there had been struggles and even excommunication, it seemed to be a case of cause and effect. Then came changes in the Church and the election of Pope John XXIII, completely different from his predecessors. Paul VI was quite different too. 'If this revelation had not happened' wrote Vintilia Horia 'all these changes, these humiliations, this eagerness to complete everything in as short a space of time as possible, would be difficult to understand or accept.' Marxist atheism is indeed the clearest expression of something that definitely belongs to Antichrist. It is nothing more than hate, violence and the materialistic outlook on life which is most in opposition to the Light of Love of Christ. And then the prophecy of Fatima adds to this argument and the forces have to be held back which have a strong desire to exorcize this evil from whatever part of the world it is found.

The journey of Paul VI to Fatima seemed to be the appropriate moment to publish these sections but nothing at all appeared. Cardinal Ottaviani then denied on 11 February, that these secret parts would be published. He assured his listeners that the part published hitherto contained the most interesting part for the world as the Madonna had asked for prayer and penitence. He went into detail: 'Here lies the secret of the victory of the good over the evil, of the heavenly kingdom over the infernal rule . . . It has a lot to say about the connection between the secret of Fatima with the tremendous and difficult situation of the Church in large zones of the world where the Devil has unleashed his ire against those who are holy and divine and from where the persecutor, even in the guise of diplomacy and the gentle language of peace, tries to extend over the whole world this dominion that he already has, to ravage lands, planting crosses, gallows and prisons, but which sanctified the martyred land.'

One cannot believe that it was the Marxist world only, which was the object of the warning of Fatima. It is the materialism which has spread all over the Western world, more responsible for evil, than the blind masses, ruled by other blind people, of Marxist society. In Europe and in America, where men have more freedom to choose than under the domination of the Soviets, there is ample proof of the wish to attain one day an unbelievable self-destruction.

The Test of the Famous Secret of Fatima

The knowledge of the secret, not revealed before, seems to have become a diplomatic indiscretion which allowed a limited circle of Roman Catholic people to know of it. The things it seems were revealed like this: by the wish of John XXIII the documents, in possession of the bishop of Leiria, were communicated so that the greatest powers in the world should know about them; Washington, Moscow and London, were shown that the most important aim above anything else was to stop the nuclear experiments. The power the Pope possessed to work for peace was plentiful. His attempts to bring about peace as has been noticed, were many. It seemed to be a character of his office. Paul VI, now in office, follows the same line. It is natural to think this was because they both knew of the grave warnings which had been given.

Here is the text of the message that a journal in Stuttgart, the *News Europa*, published for the first time on 15 October 1963 under the title of 'The Future of Humanity,' under the name of L. Einrich, reported afterwards in all the newspapers of the world. The authenticity of this document has never been in doubt.

'Have no fear, little one. I am the Mother of God who speaks to you and ask you to publish the message I am going to give you to the whole world. You will find strong resistance while you do so. Listen well and pay attention to what I tell you.

'Men must be set on the right road once more. With suppliant humility, men must seek forgiveness for sins committed already and which will be committed. You wish me to give you a sign, so that everyone will accept My Words, which I am saying through you, to the human race. I have seen the Prodigy of the Sun and all believers, unbelievers, peasants, countrywomen, wise men, journalists, laics and priests, all have seen it. And now I proclaim in my Name: "A great punishment shall fall on the entire human race, not today and not tomorrow, but in the second half of the twentieth century! I have already revealed to the children Melania and Maximine at La Salette, and today I repeat it to you for the human race has sinned and has trampled down the Gift which I have made. In no part of the world is life in order, Satan rules the highest position, laying down how things should be done. He will effectually succeed in bringing his influence right up to the top of the Church; succeed in seducing the spirits of the great scientists who invent the arms, which in ten minutes could easily wipe out all humanity. He will have under his power the rulers who govern the people and will help them to make an enormous quantity of these arms. And if humanity opposes me I shall be obliged to free the arm of My Son. Now I see that God will punish man with a severity that has not been used since the Flood.

'The time of times will come and everything will come to an end if humanity is not converted, and if things remain as they are now or get worse, or get very much worse the great and powerful men will perish just as will the small and weak.

'For the Church too, the time of its greatest trial will come. Cardinals will oppose cardinals and bishops against bishops. Satan will march in their midst and there will be great changes at Rome. What is rotten will fall, never to rise again. The church will be darkened and the world will shake with terror. The time will come when no king, emperor, cardinal or bishop will await Him who will, however, come, but in order to punish according to the designs of my Father.

'A great war will break out in the second half of the twentieth century. Fire and smoke will fall from heaven, the waters of the oceans will become vapours, the scum will arise in a confused manner, and everything will sink down. Millions and millions of men will perish while this is going on and those who survive will envy the dead. The unexpected will follow in every part of the world, anxiety, pain and misery in every country. Have I seen it? The time is getting nearer and the abyss is getting wider without hope. The good will perish with the bad, the great with the small, the Heads of the Church with their faithful, and the rulers with their people. There will be death everywhere as a result of the mistakes of the unfeeling and the partisans of Satan, but when those who survive all these happenings are still alive, they will proclaim God once again and His Glory, and will serve him as in the time when the world was not so perverted.

'Go, my little one and proclaim it. For that purpose I shall always be at your side to help you.'

The most recent call to Lucia

Men were deaf then to the words of the Virgin, as they seem to be now.

But those who have eyes to see have been able to recognize that from 1917 onwards events have bound men more and more. The pattern of events have followed one another with such confusions in men's minds and decadence in all sectors, that today there are few people who are not affected by the whirlwind which is advancing. In the first appearances a war was threatened which men waged just as the Virgin had declared. But they did not listen and the Second World War broke out.

Today there is an even worse threat: a third war. But the means of destruction are radical and the minds are even more evil.

The only survivor of the three children is Lucia, and she became first a Dorothea Sister and then, in 1948, a Barefoot Carmelite. She lives in a closed convent at Coimbra. Only she can truly tell the whole story. But the Roman Curia has always preferred that she remain isolated from all contact.

But meanwhile she did not stop to think of the future of mankind with trepidation. In 1958 Padre Agostino Fuentes, who presented the case for the beatification of Francesco and Jacinta, was able to go and see her with the permission of the Pope. Lucia received him with much sadness and greatly troubled with the future of mankind. She confided a message in him as everyone would soon know about it. It was published in Marian paper *La Immaculada*, issue of January–February 1959. Here is the text:

'Father, the Madonna is very disappointed that no one considered Your message of 1917 important. Neither the good nor the bad took any notice of it. The good went on with their own lives ignoring it, and did not follow the celestial standards, in the wide road to perdition they ignored the threatened punishments.

'Believe, Father, the Lord God will punish the world very soon. The punishment will be material and imagine, Father, how many hearts will be lost if there is no prayer and no one is penitent. This is the cause of the sadness of the Madonna.

'She said to everyone that the Madonna had time and again said to her "Many nations will disappear from the face of the Earth. Godless nations will feel the whip by God Himself to punish humanity, if we, by means of Orations and the Holy Sacraments, cannot obtain the grace of their conversion." He said that the devil was attacking in the decisive battle against the Madonna, because what troubles the Immaculate Heart of Mary and Jesus is the fall of the priestly and Religious spirit. The devil knows that the religious people and the Priests, disregarding their own vocation, drag down many hearts. We are scarcely in time to hold back the punishment from heaven. We have at our disposition two most efficacious means – Oration and Sacrifice. The devil does everything he can to take men's minds from this and take away their desire for prayer. The one will save and the other destroy. But, rather, it must be said that not everyone can await a recall to prayer and Penitence neither from the Supreme Pontiff, nor from the Bishops, nor from the Parish Priests, nor from the Superiors. It is already time that everyone on his own initiative completes holy works and reforms his own life according to the Madonna. The Devil wishes to master consecrated minds, and works to corrupt those to lead other people to final impenitence; uses every trick, suggesting to people even to postpone the religious life! From this comes sterility in the Inner Life and coldness in the secular life about the renunciation of pleasure and the total sacrifice to God.

'There are two facts to be remembered concerning the sanctification of Jacinta and Francesco; the affliction of the Madonna and the vision of the inferno. The Madonna finds herself as if between two swords; on the one hand she sees obstinate humanity indifferent to the threatened punishment; and on the other hand she sees us trampling on the Holy Sacraments and despising the coming punishment remaining unbelieving, sensual and materialistic.

'The Madonna has expressly said "We are approaching the last days" and she has repeated to me three times. She declared first, that the devil has begun the final struggle; one of the two will emerge victorious or vanquished: we can be either on God's side or on that of the devil. The second time I repeat that the ultimate remedies to be given to the world are: the Holy Rosary and the devotion of the Immaculate Heart of Mary. The third time she told me that having exhausted the other means rejected by men, she offers with trepidation the last anchor of salvation: the Holy Virgin in person, her numerous appearances, her tears, messages of prophets spread all over the world. And the Madonna said that if we did not choose Him and continued to offend Him, we would not be pardoned any more.

'It is urgent that we take notice of this terrible reality. We do not want to fill the mind with fear once again, but we want to recall it for when the Holy Virgin has given maximum efficacy to the Holy Rosary and there is no problem, spiritual, national or international, which cannot be resolved by the Holy Rosary and by our sacrifices. Recited with love and devotion, consoled Mary, holding back the tears of her immaculate Heart.'

This emotive language, typical of the Roman Catholic world is, in substance, a grave warning and one that is valid for all people, the religious and also those without religion. There must be something that all the world can understand.

13

THE APPARITIONS OF LA SALETTE, GARABANDAL AND SAN DAMIANO

The maternal aspect of the Divinity is present in every religion. With us Roman Catholics the figure of the Virgin Mary is beloved to the highest degree. The Divine Mother has a maternal care for the world and is close and is quick with aid and help especially in moments of catastrophe. It is not surprising that she intervenes in so many apparitions.

Dante, Paradise XXXIII, has sublime world for the Virgin Mary and every time we re-read his works with delight. But the résumé was splendid as was that in the Revelation 12 : 1, and is rarely studied, but it does give an idea which is unequalled.

'And there appeared a great wonder in heaven; a woman clothed with the sun, and the moon under her feet, and upon her head a crown of twelve stars:' But then comes the opposite pole: 'And there appeared another wonder in heaven; and behold a great red dragon. . . .'

The struggle between Mary and the serpent is also the struggle between the good and the bad. Revelation says that the Lady would emerge victorious. In Genesis it is affirmed quite clearly:

'And I will put enmity between thee and the woman, and between thy seed and her seed; it shall bruise thy head, and thou shall bruise his heel.' (Genesis 3 : 15.)

Louis Marie Grignion de Montfort said that the final ages will be recognizable by the presence of the Virgin. This prophecy has been verified today. There has never been a time as the last hundred years in which the Virgin has revealed herself so frequently to men and her words have been given out to us.

The first appearance of the Virgin in the last century

took place on the 19 July 1830 to Catherine Labourée in the Monastery of the Daughters of Charity, Rue du Bac, Paris. They were the first revelations.

At Lourdes on 11 February 1858, the Virgin Mary appeared to Bernadette Soubirous and renewed the invitation to pray and to do penance to avoid punishment, as she had already done at La Salette (1846). But little by little she made the warning more urgent that the times were getting nearer. At Fatima (1917) her voice was graver with her warnings to penitents. We give here the best-known examples of recent years:

Vicovaro (Rome) 1931, the movement of the eyes which went on for several days and which the author saw for himself; Bonate di Bergamo 1944; Heede 1945 in north Germany; Amsterdam 1945–1950; Rome, at the Grotto of the Three Fountains 1947; Île-Bouchard 1947, Bergalla di Balestrino (Savona) 1949; Acquaviva 1950; Ribera (Agrigento) 1950; Guarcino (Frosinone) 1950; Oriolo Calabro (Cosenza) 1951; Amorosi (Benevento) 1951; Casali Contrada (Chieti) 1951; Orria (Salerno) 1952; Syracuse, the Madonna of the Tears, 1953; Pombia (Novara) 1953; Calabrò di Mileto (Cantanzaro) 1953; Cassirano (Brescia) 1953–54; Vittoria (Ragusa) 1954; Mezzo Lombardo (Trento) 1954; Colombera di Avenza (Carrara) 1954; Giarre (Catania) 1954; Reggio Emilia 1956; Assoro (Enna) 1956; Rocca Corneta di Lizzano in Belvedere (Bologna) from 1957 to 1972; Valla Maio (Frosinone) 1958; Scheggia (Perugia) 1959; Craveggia (Novara) 1961; 'The Little Fountain' at Montichiari (Brescia) 1947–1966; S. Damiano di Piacenza from 1961 to 1972.

We also give some from other countries: Poutmain (1871) San Sebastian de Garabandal (1961–5); Svanovke, to Marietta Becò of Belgium (1932); to Banneux (1933); to Pomriazkin, Sursk, and Skiemonys (1962); Velykiai (1964).

Revelations and messages have also been received at the present time by various elect minds and passed on in love by those who see humanity going in a wrong direction.

The fundamental warning is a cry from the heart and the mother's care for her children, inviting them to penitence, exhorting them to prayer, to a moral life, counselling them to penitence, and thus saving humanity from the punishment which always follows evil works.

The prophecies of Jonah were not followed by the punishment which had been threatened because the people of Niniveh made penitence. But Sodom and Gomorrah were destroyed by the catastrophe which had been threatened, despite the warnings of Abraham.

I. *The Apparitions of La Salette*

Two little shepherdesses, Maximine Giraud (11) and Mélanie Calvat (15) were taking the cows to pasture in the mountains of the little commune of La Salette to the south of Grenoble in France 1,800 metres high. Towards midday on 19 September 1846 they went towards a little spring where they hoped to eat their simple lunch of bread and cheese.

While they were going down the mountain, they saw in a place far below them a highly luminous ball of light; it seemed as if 'the sun had fallen there'. And behold the globe opened and in front of their eyes a human form appeared. The figure took the form of a 'beautiful lady' 'all light and flowers' and sat on the stones of the fountain her elbows on her knees her head between her hands in a posture of sadness and tears. The two small children were terrified, while the 'beautiful lady' got up; she was tall and majestic. They saw that she remained suspended in the air without touching the ground, two luminous haloes were around her head, and her white habit was shining with pearls. But her face was sad. She spoke and said things that the children did not understand at first.

We quote the part of the Message which is concerned with the present and the future, leaving out that which dealt with the past. After the part where she deplores the dissolute life of the clergy, their love of money, their ambition and their irreverent celebrations of the Divine Mysteries, the Message goes on :

'France, Italy, Spain and England will be at war. Blood will flow on the streets, Frenchman will fight Frenchman and Italian against Italian and in the end will come a war that will be terrible.

'For a period of time God will not remember Italy or France for they will have forgotten the Gospel. The evil ones will display all their malice and there will be murders even in houses. At the first blow of the sword of God which will fall, like lightning on humanity, the mountains and all nature will tremble because the disorder and the misdeeds of man will rise to the vault of the sky.

'Paris will be destroyed by fire and Marseilles will be inundated by the sea, other great cities will be destroyed by fire and razed to the ground by fire. The just will have to suffer much : their prayers, penitence and tears will rise to heaven; all the people of God will pray for pardon and sing misericords, and they will come to Me for My intercession and My help. . . . There will be reconciliation between God and Man and peace. They will serve, adore and glorify Jesus Christ : love will blossom everywhere. The new rulers will be the right arm of the Holy Church, which will be strong, humble, pious, poor, fervent and a perfect imitator of the virtue of Jesus Christ. The Gospel will be preached everywhere and men will make great progress in the faith because there will be union between the workers for Jesus Christ and all who live in the fear of God.

'But this peace will not last for long; twenty-five years of plenty will be almost forgotten and the sins of men will be the cause of all the punishment which will once again be meted out to Earth.

A forerunner of Antichrist, who will lead the troops drawn from all nations, will fight against the true Christ, the only Saviour of the world. He will shed much blood in eradicating the cult of the living God and by taking His place. Then will be seen many types of punishment on Earth besides the disease and hunger which will be universal. Wars will follow wars and the final one will be led by one of the ten kings of Antichrist who will have only one will and will be the only ones to rule in the world.

'Before this event the world will have apparent peace and people will think of nothing else but pleasure and the bad ones will commit sins of all kind. But the sons of the Holy Church, the sons of Faith, My perfect imitators, will grow in the love of God and in all virtue, under the guide of the Holy Spirit. I will fight on their side until they arrive at the fullness of time.

'For the evil done by men even Nature will cry out and earthquakes will occur in protest against those who have committed crimes on Earth. The Earth will tremble and you yourselves will also tremble if you, who are dedicated to the service of Jesus Christ, and yet inside yourselves only admire yourselves. Tremble! The Lord is on the point of giving you into the hands of your enemies, inasmuch as the holy places are contaminated by corruption. Many convents are no longer the houses of God, but pastures of "Asmodeus", that is of the devil, impurity and their followers.

'Thus the time will be reached in which Antichrist will be born of a Jewish nun, a false virgin who will have intimate relations with the ancient serpent, the master of luxury. His father will be a bishop. As soon as he is born he will have teeth and pronounce blasphemies; in a word he will be a born devil. He will emit fearful cries, work miracles and wallow in luxury and impurity. He will have brothers who are demons incarnate as he will be, but sons of evil, and at the age of twelve years they will distinguish themselves in brilliant victories. Almost all of them will be the head of an armed force, supported by the infernal legions.

'The seasons will change their characteristics, the Earth will be lit with a fiendish reddish light; the water and the fire will cause terrible seismic movements which will engulf mountains and cities.

'Rome will lose the Faith and become the seat of Antichrist. The demons allied to Antichrist will operate on the Earth and in the sky and Humanity will become worse. But God will not give up his truly faithful servants who are men of good will. The Gospel will be preached everywhere to all the people and the nations will know the truth.

'I make an urgent appeal to the whole universe; I call the true disciples of God who live and reign in the sky! I use my voice as the perfect imitator of the Word Incarnate, Christ, the only Saviour of men. I warn my sons, those truly devoted to Me, who are faithful to Me because they lead me to My Son, whom I carried in My arms and Who lives always in My Spirit. Lastly, I appeal to the apostles of the last days, the disciples faithful to Jesus Christ who wait for the rule Mélanie will receive for them, who lead a life despising the world and themselves and who live in sight of a world in poverty and humility, in silence and in self-effacement, in continual prayer and in mortification, in love and in union with God in concealment and in suffering.

'The time has come that you should show yourselves to lighten the world. Go and show yourselves, my beloved sons. I am with you and in you. While your faith is the light which will help you in these days of disappointment your zeal will give you fame in the glory of Christ.

'Fight, Sons of light, you small number who see, because the time of times, the final end, is near.

'The Church will be in the dark, the world will be convulsed but in this confusion Enoch and Elijah will appear full of the spirit of God. They will preach and in their words will be the power of God and men of good will will believe in God and many spirits will be consoled, in virtue of the Holy Spirit they will make great progress and condemn the diabolical errors of Antichrist.

'Woe to the inhabitants of the Earth! There will be sanguinary war, hunger, pestilence and epidemics, terrible rains of insects, thunder which will shake entire cities, earthquakes which will make entire regions uninhabitable. Voices will be heard in the air, and men will strike their heads against the wall, wishing for death, but this will bring them, for their part, terrible torture. Blood will flow everywhere. Who could ever report victory unless God shortened the time of trial?

'Enoch and Elijah will be put to death; pagan Rome will be destroyed and fire will fall from heaven destroying three cities. The sun will be darkened and only the Faith will survive.

'The time is at hand. The abyss is opening: the king of the kings of darkness is watching, the beast is watching with his subjects who will proclaim him "saviour of the world." He will rise into the air superbly to reach the sky, but the breath of the Archangel Michael will kill him. He will fall back and the earth will shake without ceasing for three days. It will then open its womb full of fire and the beast and his followers will be allowed into the eternal abyss of the inferno. Then water and fire will purify the earth to destroy all human pride and everything will be renewed.'

After this prophecy the Madonna gave to Mélanie the Rule of the new order of the apostles and disciples of the last days and then added: 'If humanity is converted, stones and rocks will become fertile and produce grain, and the fields will give abundant harvests.'

II. *The Apparitions of Garabandal*

San Sebastian de Garabandal is a village which has about seventy families, ninety kilometres from Santander in Spain. Four children, Conchita, Maria Dolores, Jacinta and Maria Cruz had a vision of the Virgin of Carmel in June 1961. The apparition took place again on 8 December 1964 when it 'called' Conchita in a phrase to tell her what was her fortune for her name-day. [Note by translator: In Catholic countries the name-day, that is the day of the saint with the same name as oneself is as important as one's actual birthday.] She also had visions of the Archangel Michael. At Garabandal a public miracle was promised and a great punishment for humanity if it did not see the error of its ways. The great miracle would convert a lot of unbelievers and would make a breach of their rational beliefs.

A Grand and Spectacular Miracle

'There will be first a warning and then a grand miracle.' But let us see what Conchita herself has written:

The Warning. 'The Virgin told me this on 1 January 1965 at Pini. I cannot tell exactly what she said as she ordered me not to do so. She did not tell me when it would happen and thus I do not know. Yes, I know that it will be visible all over the world, it will be the direct work of God and will take place before the miracle. I do not know if anyone will die. But my impression is that some will die.'

The mother of Conchita has revealed after being informed by her daughter that the 'Warning' will coincide with the outbreak of revolution in Spain.

The Miracle. 'The Virgin has told me alone what I know about the miracle. She has forbidden me to say what form it will take and I can say the date only eight days before. What I can say is that it will coincide with the feast of a holy martyr of the Eucharist; that it will occur at 20.30 on a Thursday; that it will be visible to all the people who are in the village of Garabandal or the surrounding mountains; the sick who see it will be cured and the unbelievers will believe. It will be the greatest miracle that Jesus has ever performed in the world. There will be no doubt that it will come from God and that it will be for the benefit of humanity. A trace of the miracle will remain at Pini for ever. It will be able to be filmed and appear on television.'

The Punishment. 'The punishment will take place if humanity does not do what it is told by the warning by the Virgin Mary and the Miracle. If it comes, I know what form it will take because the Virgin has told me, but I cannot say. Furthermore, I have seen the punishment. Yes, I can assure you that it is worse than if one were surounded by fire; worse than if one had fire above and below one. I do not know how long it will be before God sends it after having performed the miracle.'

In January 1965 Conchita had this further warning: '... for those who have survived the new reign of God will be established, and humanity will turn and serve it just as in the time before the perversion of the world ... What a misfortune if this conversion does not take place, and everything will have to remain as at the present moment or if the responsibility got even worse.'

This took place in the apparition of 18 June 1965.

Message Given to the World by the Virgin by means of the Archangel Michael

'Because my Message of 18 October was not completed and not made known I tell you that this will be the last of them. Before the ladle can be refilled it must be first emptied. Many priests, bishops and cardinals are on the road to perdition taking many souls with them. Every day they give less importance to the Eucharist. We must avoid the anger of the good God above us with our own efforts. If we seek pardon, with a sincere mind, He will pardon us. I, your Mother, by means of the angel St. Michael want to tell you and correct you.

'You are warned for the last time. I love you a lot and do not wish to condemn you. Ask with a sincere heart and we will give it to you. You must have more spirit of sacrifice. Think of the passion of Jesus.'

The last appearance took place on 13 December 1965.

III. *At San Damiano di Piacenza*

A few kilometres away from Piacenza in the locality of San Damiano, extraordinary phenomena continue to take place to which many pilgrims, both Italian and others, can bear witness. Mamma Rosa, a woman getting on in years, simple and little known, who lives in San Damiano, was the first witness. 'Jesus has chosen you for his instrument as you are the most ignorant,' said the Virgin to her one day (it was 15 December 1967). She was to be the means by which warnings were to be given. They are facts given beforehand with the tone of maternal love which advises a change in the way of life before punishment. It is the language which can be accepted by those against whom it is spoken. We select from the various messages which Mamma Rosa receives every Friday and transmits to the crowds which come here from all parts of the world.

'When I see the anxiety, the darkness and the weeping, raise your eyes to heaven call me by the sweet name of Mother and I will see you, embrace you and will carry you to the heavenly country; there you will sing with Angels and Saints; there you will have pardon and all will be saved in so much joy and where we make a great feast.' (9 June 1967.)

'All that you will have supported in the name of Jesus will be written in the Book of Gold.' (13 August 1967.)

'There will be 100 years or more before I shall be on this earth to awaken the hearts of my sons to save them, help them and to give them so much faith and so much love ...' (10 December 1968.)

'Do not be discouraged, but I shall come soon with the Light! So many signs will be seen in the sky and on earth ... sufficient to make you believe! Everything will be done to save you, I will give the means to everyone, and help everyone.' (10 December 1968.)

'The world is in mud: it does not understand the truth of God any longer. They want to ignore the truth, they want to go alone.' (5 May 1967.)

'The world is being lost little by little ... they do not accept my invitation.' (25 May 1967.)

'Always add to your faith because the moments will become terrible. You see in many parts of the world many shocks, many disasters, earthquakes. Pray, pray with Faith as the Eternal Father has piety.' (15 August 1967.)

'You have not listened to my word as Mother ... but when terrible things happen, will it be your fault as you have not chosen my word?' (4 August 1967.)

'Pray for pardon to the Eternal Father who has piety and misericord, because the terrible scourges are really terrible, to an extent which cannot be imagined.' (9 January 1967.)

'The heavenly Mummy says now: Presto! She leaves and goes to other seers all over the world, yes, also in Russia.' (15 August 1965.)

'The Eternal Father has given this comfort after the war to nations all over the place ... and this comfort they have cast into the mud, not to thank Jesus and Mary. They have only done acts of pride and vanity.' (9 June 1967.)

'From one moment to another, you can be on the threshold of terrible tribulations.' (10 December 1966.)

'When you feel great shocks, when you see great darkness, raise your eyes to heaven holding your hands wide apart, ask for piety and misericords, recite the Salve Regina, recite the Creed.' (22 May 1967.)

'When you see what day the sky will open, there will be a terrible struggle of anxiety and weeping ... But do not fear, recite the Creed. Pray to the Archangel Michael with his crown between his hands that he give you strength, courage in the struggle to be saved on Earth and enjoy the eternal happiness in Heaven ... I with your guardian Angel with St. Michael Archangel ... You are helping minute by minute, do not worry about it ... Pray, pray, pray always with a smile on your lips. Those who have to leave this Earth will arrive in Heaven with a great array of angels and will travel over the world to comfort, pray, and raise the spirits of all the brothers.' (22 November 1967.)

'You must do everything to console the minds as the hour of the terrible punishment has struck ... the warning has sounded; you must understand that it is the beginning of terrible trials of anxiety and tears ... We are already 130 years after La Salette and 50 years after Fatima, and three years here. Do not wait for the hour to sound, love one another; carry love in your hearts. Not pride, not conceit, but only love and peace in the heart. Then when the terrible moments of darkness come you will have Jesus in your heart, you will be strong. He will await until the very last hour, believe me.' (9 June 1967.)

'The hour has sounded, the hour has sounded, the Eternal Father will not delay any longer, but keep on praying and with me we can intercede with prayer and sacrifice.' (5 August 1967.)

'What will become of you if you do not come here to take force, courage, faith to resist all struggles, tribulations, crosses, persecutions, wars, earthquakes, illness and hunger; if you do not have strength and resistance, what will become of you?' (9 June 1967.)

'For those who have faith, and to those everything is possible, it is the promise of aid, of help, becoming real certainties of the greatest strength. I come into your midst ... Do not fear. Go forward, do not wait for a ferocious war to break out in the world so savage that no one will be saved.' (12 September 1967.)

'I will come with great power and give light to all.' (6 October 1967.)

'... I will open the eyes of all, in the entire world with a very strong light.' (23 December 1966.)

'It is I who wish to save you who am your Mother,

your advocate, your teacher, your Mother ... who loves you a lot.' (31 December 1969.)

'I am come down of Earth to bring joy, concord and consolation among families.' (30 December 1966.)

'There will be numerous signs in the sky by day and by night, before the tribulation comes.' (30 October 1966.)

'... there will not only be signs on earth there will be signs in the sky ... signs of preparations on high that Jesus has given to prepare the minds for my coming.' (21 June 1967.)

'Those who come in faith will all receive a sign.' (4 March 1966.)

'When you see a great sign in heaven, it will be the great and terrible moment ... of anxiety and pain. (13 January 1967.)

'A star will come in the sky ... I will come among you in that star ... and I will give light to the entire world ... I will give so many signs in the sky, in the Moon in the Sun, in the stars and in many places, about my coming.' (7 April 1967.)

(In a message in 1961 the Virgin at San Damiano said: 'Watch the sky, watch it often for a very bright star with a long tail ... when you see it, in the evening or the morning ... unexpectedly – and it will appear in many regions – it will be a sign of calamity.')

'Watch the sky, watch it often: you will find signs there and when you see a grand sign (the Cross in the sky) the moment will be grave and anxious. Pray ... because I will come to the entire world in triumph with a great light and my Son Jesus will come with a New Reign and will bring peace, love, tranquility and joy in men's hearts. (13 May 1967.)

'... the cloud will advance from every part of the Earth and the minds which have not the Light will perish and the people will fear who live in a profound "sleep".

'The sickle will come and will exterminate them inexorably all over the world. I have blessed all the sons faithful to this Heart which is so much adored. When you see the clouds of the Divine revenge pray and invoke My Name which is the Power in the minds of goodwill. Carry My Name all the time in your heart and it will be your defence against the infernal hurricane which awaits you: Thus it is written in Heaven ... The gangrene of the people will be torn in pieces, unbelievable to the human eye. The Vatican will be covered with calumnies, but will already know it has dear sons. What is crumbling will fall and a New Age will arise. My large Mantle will cover all those who have suffered so much. ... The enemy will fly from the Cross and go and take his rest among those who will torture people to death; but you, oh, sons of the Cross, will enjoy the Aurora of the New Age: Thus it is written in Heaven.' (25 March 1970.)

'The Archangel Michael says: "Go! Go! Speak! ... I with my sword and you with Rosary in your hand ... Do not wait the terrible moment! The hour has struck! ... The Mother of Heaven has already announced it. Now I am sent in Her Name to announce it too! It is the hour of awakening. And I will light you, protect you, and defend you with my sword, in the name of all the angels and saints. You will be surrounded and no one will be able to harm you! Advance! Advance! Triumph with Jesus and Mary!"' (5 January 1968.)

'I want all Nations under my Mantle. No one will then be lost, they are all my children.' (5 January 1968.)

14

THE MOST RECENT PROPHECIES
ON THE FUTURE OF HUMANITY

We will glean from the many other predictions of astrologers, seers and prophets what they have foreseen by writing or talking of the future.

Russia and the United States Allied against China

The war, which has been going on for a number of years in Vietnam between Russia and China on the one hand against the United States, [Note by translator: the original Italian version of this book was written before the Cease-fire in Vietnam on 28 January 1973] will lead to a change of alliances – according to some prophets – in the sense that Russia and China will become hostile to each other. Others say, like E. Cayce, M. de Sabato and others, that the Russians and the Americans will be allies in a future war against China. But this is wrong. The Chinese will bring about the greatest invasion that history has ever recorded: all Europe will be occupied. The conflict will start by skirmishes on the frontier, then the 800 million Chinese will overflow their confines in a number of directions. One part will go towards Japan and another towards the west. The first victims will be Indochina, India, Pakistan, Afghanistan, Iran, Russia, Syria, Turkey and then Greece, which will be overrun one by one. The Communist countries of Europe will be overthrown one after the other. The horde will then attack Austria and Germany, then it will be the turn of Italy and Switzerland as far as Belgium and Holland. Then it seems there will be a pause along a line which will go from Holland via Geneva, Lyon and the present France-Italian frontier as far as Mentone. But France and Switzerland will sign a treaty of peace with the

Chinese and will be evacuated by the yellow forces. In the other occupied countries there will be stories of cruelty, rape and bloodshed except in Albania, allied to the Chinese.

The astrologer Mario de Sabato is the one who made this prediction. He goes on to say that Europe will reorganize itself after this and victors and vanquished will end up as friends.

The Great Exodus

In a book published by Mario de Sabato called *Confidences of a Seer*, the author writes:

'It will begin with fighting between India and China, and will last, on the other hand, for a considerable time, with periods of peace. Then one day the great blow will fall, the great parting and China will emerge from her frontiers . . .' in the direction which we have said. It will be a river of hundreds of millions of men, 'a great exodus', as De Sabato calls it, 'not conditioned, often without arms, as if the invaders were coming to Europe to take riches for themselves. It is very rare to see one country rise against three continents. No one will be at the side of China in her expansion except a small European country' (Albania?)

'This war will present a very grave economic problem for Europe. It will be treated as a true world revolution. The man who exists within the superficial man will be drawn towards other men as a result of the fear and the cruelty.

'But the Chinese, who will have abandoned their country will continue to expand over the world, above all in Europe. Then will come the cross-breeding of the races and the reorganization of Europe and of Asia.'

The epoch of this end of the world will be, for him, the decade 1972–82 in which will be wars and invasions. Then there will be world agreement and Europe and Asia will become Eurasia, after which the true golden age will begin. This will be formed of three periods: the first, progressist, of 170 years; the second, prophetic, of 370 years; the third, apocalyptic, of 190 years. There will be 730 years of peace and well-being under wise rulers, who will bring about the religious and political union of the people. During the prophetic period (370 years) men will receive visits from people from other planets and the inhabitants of the Earth will be able to travel in space.

How will it affect Italy

The prophecies of Mario de Sabato about how the next few years will affect Italy can be summed up in this way:

The country will be shaken by troubles, political crises and lack of government very often and for long periods. Economic crises with strikes will occur to complicate the situation of disorder. There will be an uprising following the formation of a provisional government. This will be of the left, but not communist. There will be important reforms.

Italy will emerge from the crises and become a very rich country with the highest possible standards of living.

Unfortunately there will be vexations from natural catastrophes tidal waves and floods, particularly in the north in Lombardy and also in Venice, where the situation will be very grave.

'A tidal wave will do considerable damage in the city just at the moment when the place is being restored . . . But despite that, Venice will be saved.'

There will be other earthquakes beside that one and they will be in central Italy in the region of Terni, Orvieto, Ansedonia, Tarquinia, Tuscania and Chianciano.

There will be disorders in the regions and incidents in Sardinia, Calabria, Sicily and Piedmonte.

Italian scientists will make an important discovery of a cure for cancer and a grave epidemic will affect the whole country.

There will be discord between the Catholic Church and the Italian government. Divorce will be much easier in Italy and the same change will have already been made in other countries.

The Red Flag fluttering over the Vatican

Gloomy predictions about future years are given in numerous messages of a Capucin monk who is a seer, Fra Giorgio Maria da Terni who lives at Todi (Perugia). We will quote some of them.

'During the centuries many Priests, Bishops, Cardinals, Popes have given a bad example adding to the despair of the faithful and their perplexity and even succeeding in compromising them with the sons of darkness. Let us rejoice as the Kingdom of God is near! But we are at the last days of dominion by Satan, who before his relegation with his followers into the eternal abyss, will have his dominion from 1973 to 1985. Today not even St. Francis could avoid the total collapse of the world and of the Church.'

'All the prophecies of the Gospels, the Saints, the Martyrs amply confirm that the present generation is that which will see the end of the world. In 1972 Paul VI ascended the Papal throne settling the Schism in the Church. From 1973 to 1975 there will be hecatombs not only in Italy but also in Europe. At Christmas 1973, announced by a terrible whirlwind on the Alban Hills, and as a result of a conspiracy, the lily of Paul VI will be bloodstained and he will render his soul to God. Naples and a number of other coastal cities will be completely destroyed by tremendous naval bombardments. Beginning with Rome, pillaged and sacked, scourged with pestilence and fire, numberless savage hordes will pour into it one after the other, Russians, Slavs, French, Spanish, Israelis, Arabs, Chinese. Thirty million Italians will be massacred and eliminated by appalling atrocities.' (Easter 1971.)

'The Red Flag will flutter over the Vatican. God's

punishment on Rome will be announced by an earthquake much stronger than that at Golgotha. The opening of the sluice gates at the junction of the Anio and Tiber rivers will flood all Valmelaina, the Tufello, Montesacro, the Salario, the Nomentano, the historical centre of Rome, Trastevere, Trionfale, and Prati. On the Esquiline Hill the muddy torrent will reach the first floor of the houses. But Ostia Lido, Monteverde Vecchio and Monteverde Nuovo, Parioli, Montemario, the villages round the periphery and Primavalle will be undamaged. There will be a thirst for blood and a vendetta. All the Catholics will be spared but in the chaos there will be no electric light, no refurnishing, radio or television. They will be preserved from death, thirst, hunger, provided that they had blessed the candle of God beforehand, lighting them in front of the Holy Images. Then comes the end of the scourge, the pestilence, inexorable and undisputed. All Lazio will be destroyed at the savage order of Gog and Magog who will land at Nettuno. An imaginary panorama over Europe would show that in Spain Madrid, San Sebastian, Cadiz and Barcelona have been put to fire and sword. In France Paris has been burned down, and in Switzerland Geneva has been swallowed into the earth. Austria and West Germany will be invaded by East Germany, supported by Russian tanks.' (May 1971.)

The Years of the Fat Cattle and the Lean Cattle

A. Barbault, in his book *The Stars and History* affirms that the actual chaotic era will last until 1992, because not until then will the Earth be affected by Uranus. He predicts imminent tribulations for 20 years, beginning in 1972.

The years from 1965 to 1971 will be considered the seven years of the fat cattle, of general well-being, which will be followed by just as many years of lean cattle, 1972 to 1978. The year 1972 is counted among the worst that humanity has ever seen. Indeed, that year will see the beginning of the Third World War which will be the worst of all time. The total of dead and ruins will be more than those of past wars which by comparison will be considered to have had little effect on the life of men. There will be groups of peoples struggling against one another. This chaos will be provoked by Neptune and his three oppositions in the astrological sky from 1971 onwards. With the year 1971 will begin the universal conversion to bolshevism which for a decade will be the calamity which will change the entire planet. They will be years of ruin and destruction. The Arabs will give a hand in this damage against Italy, France and Spain which will become communist colonies for a time. The invaders, as well as other evils, will bring cholera, typhoid, pestilence and famine. *The whole Afro-Asian world will be against Europe*, helped by well-meaning but misguided church people in Europe.

The disorder and the chaos will thus include the church, with the abdication of Pope Montini by the laws he himself promulgated.

According to other prophets, the Third World War will break out after the assassination of a great statesman in the direction of Hungary or Yugoslavia. A nun who helps Jacinta (of Fatima) has declared that the Third World War will break out around 1972.

The crisis of 1972 will be more Italo-German than Franco-British. The triple triangle of 1973 will be favourable to the bad influences. In 1973 the lira will be devalued more than the mark in 1924 with all the consequences of disorder and revolt because of the soaring rise in prices and the complete ruin of many people. With the red invasion Europe will be in total desolation. Thus we arrive at 1975, the year of the 'Tempest of the Cross' of Mandorlo Fiorito, during which nine-tenths of the Earth will be dominated by Moscow (including Australia and Canada).

As far as Rome is concerned, the worst period will be in 1975–7 when a flood without precedent will take place which will cause damage and casualties almost beyond number. The lowering of moral standards will have their nadir in 1975–7. 'Those who gave alms will receive them.'

From 1975 things will get worse, but a true reconstruction will not follow because shortly afterwards another war will break out. In 1978 life will have to begin all over again after so much destruction. Isolated revolts against the communist devastators will take place from 1980 onwards. A Fourth World War, almost exclusively Chinese, will break out that year, it will mainly concern Asia, which after the tremendous destruction and massacre which has taken place in Europe, comprises three-quarters of the inhabitants of the Earth. The two colossi which will face each other are India and China. There will be neither victors nor vanquished, but China will engulf many parts of India.

In the fifteen years between 1988 and 2003 A. Barbault foresees the check of the Communists and the coming of the forces which will defeat them, especially after 1993. The theatre for this struggle will be especially in the Far East. After the chasing of the barbarians, the Europe of 1990 will be largely isolated from respectable and civilized life. The last decade of the century (1990–9) will be reasonably tranquil, but before 1989 he says there will have to be three world wars so appalling that they make previous conflicts seem mild by comparison.

After so many struggles and cataclysms, Humanity will be able to enjoy an epoch of peace. But, nevertheless this tranquility is only a prelude to taking up war and fighting on a larger scale which will precede the appearance of Antichrist who will bring major ruin.

Will the Axis of the Earth be Changed Suddenly?

Edgar Cayce, one of the greatest prophets, has predicted the end of Communism in Russia, which, allied to the U.S.A., will become the hope of the new society, founded not on fighting, but on world collaboration.

After the oppression of the tsar, these working people have passed to another extreme; they will not be able to have peace without freedom of expression and until they are deprived of the most elementary rights of man among which is the right to profess his religion according to the dictates of his conscience. The attempt to 'level not only the economic life but also the mental and spiritual welfare as well, will not last very long,' being profoundly evil and therefore destined to fail, and a cause of suffering to the man who is not considered as a human being but as a numeral. This is also true for all people opposed to a regime of moral and material violence, Communist, Fascist, or Nazi. 'When one forgets to love one's neighbour, the Lord cannot have clemency, and this situation cannot last long.'

He predicts that China will not only become democratic, but that Christianity will be largely spread in that sub-continent, too.

The exceptional qualities as a prophet with which E. Cayce was endowed have been proved by innumerable facts and people run to him. The greater part of his replies are given while he is lying on a bed in a state of trance. He seems to be reading a book then which is open in front of him. He makes diagnoses, gives cures, reads into the future and the past with an incredible clarity and simplicity, so much so that his replies are called 'lectures'. He has been subjected to numerous proofs and tests, and many doctors from all parts of the United States consult him.

Cayce has repeatedly declared that the terrestrial axis began to change in 1936. There will be a gradual movement of the poles. This in fact, when it begins to speed up will have catastrophic consequences. If the Nations succeed in avoiding a Third World War, it is possible that a cataclysm will transform life on Earth. An inclination of the Earth's axis would change the seasons and could provoke enormous disasters. The changing of the climate would make a new Ice Age inevitable with all its consequences. It would bring tremendous ruin. Cayce has predicted the almost total destruction of Los Angeles and San Francisco first, and later on, New York. These disasters will form part of a world catastrophe during the period before the end of the century 'when a new millennium full of hope will begin'.

In January 1934 he forecast: 'The Earth will open in the western part of the Japanese islands which will sink into the sea. Northern Europe will be changed in the twinkling of an eyelid. A new country will appear off the east coast of America.'

A well-known American geologist declared that the drastic changes forecast by Cayce could be attributed to the change of the rotation of the axis, begun below the surface of the Earth as said above, in 1936.

Speaking of Atlantis, E. Cayce describes its splendour and its ruin, confirming that the last islands disappeared under the waters of the Caribbean about ten thousand years ago. He forecast that one day this land would come to the surface once more.

The Messages of Borup

The inspired prophetic utterances attributed to Borup in Denmark seem to be the same version, though in modern idiom of the announcement in the Bible of the end of the world. Indeed he speaks of atomic war (fire which comes from the sky), landings by beings from outer space, that Jesus will come down in clouds with angels (flying saucers), that some will be taken away on high, of the purification of the Earth, and then the New Heaven and the New Earth after 'the great and terrible day of the Lord' (Malachi 4 : 5) as it is called by that prophet. Indeed, more than the events which will precede the last day, these communications refer to what is happening now and what will happen immediately afterwards.

Concerning the time there are no details as to which year will be the decisive one, but very significant agreement with other Christian prophecies. (Nostradamus, St. Malachi, Garabandal, Fatima, etc) which predict the end about the year 2000. In addition to this, those who draw their conclusions from the study of the Pyramids and the astrologers who read the stars, have fixed a time a little after 2000. But we prefer to believe in the affirmation of Him Who said 'But as for the day and the hour, no-one knows it, neither the angels in heaven nor the Son, but only the Father.' In these prophetic messages it is said that 'everything will come to pass in the twentieth century as predicted and suddenly when it comes'. They declare also that our calendar is thirteen years behind. We are at the eleventh hour, the eve of the fulfilment of everything that has been forecast in the centuries which have gone before.

All the outward signs show that this end is near. The events which have taken place in these last years are the beginning of the events which have been foreseen. The things which seem cruel to many are a natural process as Man with his mistakes has created by himself the cause of all the disasters which are to come. The greatest mistake he has made is to have destroyed the microcosm. Among other things, Man has violated the laws by disintegrating the atom. Microcosm and macrocosm are firmly bound together.

The Consequences of the Errors

Man has gone so far that he cannot continue along the road he has taken and survive at the same time. It will result in calamities more terrible because it will lead to a general atomic war accompanied by unbelievable sufferings. Terrestrial science put at the service of egoism has reached such power that massacre can be carried out to perfection. Science has advanced so far today that Man has not reached the spiritual maturity to control it. It has reached the level beyond which it cannot advance, it has reached the point where it has overcome the spirit. Man is capable of wiping himself out and destroying the whole surface of the planet. He could even harm the galaxy to which he belongs. But this will not happen.

The greatest danger in the human state is that of possessing power to contaminate the entire Earth and to harm the other inhabitants of space. Because of this the end of the world is near.

Man will be allowed to achieve all that he has invented ignoring the superior laws, to go on hating himself and to be struck by the hate by which he has surrounded himself on all sides.

The consequences of these actions will fall on those who have carried them out. Thus the situation in which Man finds himself bound is like a road without a way out at the bottom of which is written 'Self-destruction'.

The reaction is quite natural, because it returns man to where he started. This concept is undoubtedly superior to that usual among those who have the Jewish concept of the anger and revenge of God. By his freedom Man can reach his own limits but not as far as endangering the lives of other worlds.

What will happen is the fulfilment of the law. In the Gospel it is said that it must be avenged. Humanity will wake and understand only when it finds itself in a situation without a way out.

We can be saved by the aid which will come to stop the total destruction and to save those who will form the New Humanity. Only with this help from above can Man get out of his situation. But the help will come only when asked for and when man has arrived at the limit of his self-destructive folly. If it were not asked for or not accepted it would be interference and thus violation of free choice.

Those who will come and bring help are a grade higher in the scale of life and hierarchy. The universe is infinitely large and Man ignores even the number of the galaxies. Forms of life can be found there which we cannot see, hear or imagine. There are other places in outer space where evolution has taken place harmoniously. To this is added a superior conscience. There something has happened which has not happened on Earth and it has advanced further. Man has instead abused his position of knowledge to advance along certain lines and remain backward in other essential points. Other beings in thousands of years have reached the stage in which Man will be in three thousand years. Thus the inhabitants of Venus have a superior conscience to that of Man on Earth. They understand and follow the Law. They can also fly in Space. Man has only just learned to do this. [Note by translator: the original remark here has been superceded by events.]

They are beings which have the capacity to assume physical form and then to dissolve again, being much more highly advanced than Man as they live on the principal of love and as elder brothers are ready to run to help those who need it.

'We are', they say, 'dual people, that is we are material and spiritual, and we can show ourselves in two ways.' They affirm that they have come in contact with many men, spiritually, that is telepathically, to have approached others in a completely physical way, and to have invited on Earth inhabitants of Space already who walk around among men. But they are self-disciplined and do not interfere in any way with human life here.

Little by little the events speed up there will be great suffering but every man will be enabled to see from a spiritual point of view.

In the near future, before the end of the century, a number of flying saucers will appear and they will be seen with increasing frequency. Everyone will see them. To see entire squadrons of them will become a normal occurrence. They will be part of the events which will occur before the Great Day. Demonstration flights will take place when the political situation on the Earth is such that a global war cannot be avoided. They will be demonstration flights which will serve many objects, but the most important is to make Man realize that there are beings of a higher state of development than his wretched struggles.

All this has been accurately forecast and nothing has been forgotten under the surveillance of the great Spirit of the Hierarchy.

The presence of the flying saucers is a truth which has a highly moral significance and consequence for the hierarchic Law for which the beings, besides seeking to raise themselves even higher, help those who are their inferiors without interfering in their affairs and having absolute respect for their free choice and their independence.

The Dramatic Announcement of the Events

'The Chinese people is actually the factory of power which will break the balance of power on Earth. The world is moving towards an atomic war which in its extreme consequences will signify the extinction of all life on this globe. It does not seem possible to avoid the catastrophe ... Suddenly,' continue the Messengers, 'the great events in the world will speed up. This will have its origin in China and will spread towards Russia and Europe until the world becomes an inferno.' 'It will all start with a war in the Far East which will degenerate rapidly into an atomic war.'

The language is clear, unequivocal and has no uncertainty of what is said. But among all this horror there is a hope. A science and a technology more advanced are ready to help men, above all by their higher development and the sense of altruism of being on a higher plane and interested in what is going on in the whole Universe.

'We,' declare those giving the message, 'are called to make immediate and intense preparations for aid on a gigantic scale which at a predetermined moment, during the trials that humanity is inflicting on itself, will come from Outer Space. And the things which will come into action are the flying saucers, they will help in the evacuation on a grand scale by means of teletransport on space ships. There will be mass landings when "the point of no return" is reached and someone in a desperate situation prepares to "press the button".'

The Great Day

No flesh could survive those days if they are not shortened. The night of Gethsemane is the tremendous image of human suffering in those atrocious hours. Many will die suddenly. But the suffering cannot last too long.

'When the desperation shall be at its highest, we shall come from space in a way which humanity will be able to understand: People will be able to see us, feel us and be able to find us. We will act as a lamp from one second to another.

'Who listens and obeys will be raised in the air and from there will help in the purification of the Earth by fire. After this they will be taken back on Earth and will continue their life in a new spirit.

'We will evacuate in mass those who remain on Earth receiving them in huge space ships which have been specially built for the purpose.'

'People who suffer, the ill, the injured and also the crippled, those ill from birth and others will be cured and become perfectly normal after entering into space ships: this will be a consequence of the Karmic Purification of the Earth and the principle of Grace will be carried into effect.'

'While the purification takes place, those who have been transported in space ships will receive aid either material or spiritual to exist and then be carried back to Earth in a perfect state of health and having undergone a complete spiritual change.'

The Earth will Stop and then Oscillate

After the evacuation, the Earth will stop still for an instant. Then it will turn and then oscillate, rapid oscillation like a lamp. Then everything will be completely changed, where was sea will be land and where land was will be sea.

The surface will be purified. Everything that has been created will vanish from the thoughts of man and what has been influenced by the mistakes of conscience hitherto represented. Without this one would be exposed to influence passed on by consciousness of those who come back to Earth and everything would start again as before.

The etheric body of the Earth and the atmosphere as well would be entirely cleaned of radio-activity and from all impurity that man has brought on to it. Because of this it is so necessary to manage the force of thought with care. Words and thoughts are living things, impulses, the beginning of creation.

The New Earth will be the planet renewed, capable of being the home of men who are more advanced.

Who will be taken and who left

In the Gospel it is said that of two men one will be taken and the other left. But in most cases neither of them know the reason why.

The proofs that man is on the point of undergoing suffering are necessary for his evolution. But some will overcome it and others will not. No one will be lost however, but there will be those who do not open their eyes until the last moment.

'To overcome the tests, raising his own consciousness to a superior grade, and thus obtaining salvation, men are asked: (1) To recognize and accept of their own will the name and the existence of God; (2) To place themselves under divine laws. This is enough to save them and to continue their life on this renovated Earth. Who changes, even at the last moment, will be saved.'

That is the principle of Grace. Men will then be rehabilitated by God. There will be more joy about one sinner who repents than 99 who have not sinned. For those who realize that they have done wrong, deplore it, promising not to do it again, have attained the purpose of the lesson.

Those who do not adapt themselves to the condition of the laws are lost from the Earth, but not by God: those who have not been brought to the New Age will go on and continue their evolution elsewhere, being reincarnated on other planets which do not belong to this galaxy, and continue to live at their level for the point of view of the hierarchy in a place having the same mode of evolution as the Earth and in accordance with their actual mode of living on Earth. But these too, will sooner or later reach the following level. They will be able to learn for these thousand years but the passage will then be verified. No-one will know what has happened. The record of the past will be blotted out, no one will suffer any more but will live once more in a world of error and that will be because they wanted it like that. They have seen, acted and killed with the masses because they were incapable of acting on their own and following an independent road.

The dead continue to live with their own sufferings until they render an account that the values and the spiritual powers which all possess can be used scientifically to look for God. Then the sufferings will come to an end.

Some will obtain the annulment of their own Karma

quickly but others will continue to bear it. That depends on the bearing of each one in the situation in which he finds himself. Until they have the ability to love, they will remain in an inferior state of evolution.

Massive help will be given also on the material plane towards the reconstruction of the New Age on the New Earth that it may be achieved the more quickly.

Men who have passed the test will have a thousand years to raise themselves spiritually to the level in which a physical body is no longer necessary.

15

THE THOUSAND HAPPY YEARS ON
THE REVIVED EARTH

> *Blessed are they who are invited*
> *to the nuptial feast of the Lamb.*
> Revelation 5.

The chaining of the dragon after the bitter struggle when he was unchained in his years of freedom are imminent and will give the start for the thousand happy years during which peace will be enjoyed at last on the Earth.

At the same time in this remainder of the century he will perform a lot of work and make a lot of noise until the moment he is chained up. We will then have the first resurrection which is talked about in the Scriptures.

The First Resurrection

'And I saw an angel come down from heaven, having the key of the bottomless pit and a great chain in his hand and he laid hold on the dragon, that old serpent, which is the Devil, and Satan, and bound him a thousand years. And cast him into the bottomless pit, and shut him up, and set a seal upon him, that he should deceive the nations no more, till the thousand years should be fulfilled: and after that he must be loosed a little season.

'And I saw thrones, and they sat on them and judgement was given unto them: and I saw the soul of them that were beheaded for the witness of Jesus, and for the word of God, and which had not worshipped the beast, neither his image, neither had received his mark upon their foreheads, on in their hands; and they lived and reigned with Christ a thousand years. But the rest of the dead lived not again until the thousand years were finished.

'This is the first resurrection. Blessed and holy is he that hath part in the first resurrection: on such the second death hath no power, but they shall be priests of God and of Christ, and shall reign with him a thousand years.' (Revelation 20 : 1–6.)

The New Age

'According to the principle of the Great Week and the six days of a thousand years of the adamic Era, there will follow a day of rest, the Millennium which from the year 2001 will bring a thousand years of peace,' wrote G. Barbarin. This is the Golden Age, the eternal aspiration of men of all time for peace after the struggle, paradise on Earth dreamed of as the blessed hope during human travail, and the Biblical Seventh day in which 'God rested'. All the prophecies are remarkably in agreement on this.

The New Age is a repetition in a different form of other ages which have united their achievements before they went down in decadence. The evolutive phases repeat themselves apparently, because that which is about to come, while it is yet secret, tends to repeat itself as a phenomenon but it is not an exact repetition. Life is a divine gift which few appreciate at its full value and only a small number of people are able to appreciate the beauty in its panoramic vision.

'And I saw a new heaven and a new earth: for the first heaven and the first earth were passed away and there was no more sea.'

The material world has faded away. We are in new surroundings where the light vibrates in a diverse light and the beings are more luminous as they are more developed.

The New Humanity will be better than the present one because it will be made up of juster men who have risen above the level of animals. A stage further on the road of life.

The alteration in thought of those who have overcome the imminent tests naturally cause changes in the physical body. Thus, the development of that part of the human brain not used already will allow the practical use of the pituitary and pineal glands. Man will, therefore, be able to respond to vibrations on the astral plane and note the most subtle vibrations of thought. His ability will be thus greatly increased and he will be capable of great good, and to be able to see and feel things imperceptible to the senses today. It will be normal to be able to perceive sounds and sights which our senses cannot perceive today. Life will be enormously widened.

The meaning of space and time, prisons for men today will thus be greatly modified. All the faculties will be developed, thus men will develop up to a new plane of evolution.

The life of men will last longer. When an existence comes to an end, consciousness will change and take on another body when the time to change takes place. It will be a process of reincarnation according to a divine plan. Death will be vanquished and it will be realized that life is eternal.

All will be changed

The nervous system will be developed to make people more sensitive and able to respond to very subtle and rapid vibrations in comparison with which the sensations today would appear heavy and gross. Even at the end of the present era the people who are highest developed will be endowed with more receptive aerials. Today, on the other hand, these people, in the surroundings in which they are forced to live, feel all the disadvantages and suffer even more because their delicate nerves cannot endure shock, sudden noise, intoxication and similar gross things. Unless the surroundings are modified, this type of person cannot survive.

Hitherto a great number of men have lived little better than at the level of animals. The necessity for material existence takes up most of their activity and much of their energy. Struggles and conflicts are the consequences of these. In future, much activity carried on today, will not have to be carried on because the new society will have other ideas and ideals. Thus a large number of men in the future will have as their chief activities creative work in science and the arts. Knowledge in the field of physics, chemistry and mathematics will be much wider and deeper. From this Man will be able to take and set free beneficial forces of exceptional power for the good of all.

These forecasts of the future have been given in prophetic and inspired communications from various seers.

The Principle of Love

The men of tomorrow will record the past as we consider the cannibals and cave-men today. Thus we shall appear to the future society made up of superior men who will not have as the object of their lives money, possessions, power, pleasure and the suppression of those whom they feel are obstacles to their egotistical plans.

This poor humanity will have finally reached its ideal, that ideal which was lacking but has been forecast by Christ.

Human experience will have taught man that love and spirituality are the highest level of life, because only loving one another as oneself can result in the automatic solving of all the social problems of life on Earth. Love and the divine force will unite those who have been separated by stubbornness and selfishness. By means of this a human society could be supported by means of love alone. Those people are decadent who are not able to be born again in love, because only love is vital. Men who have already understood it and only now, have truly realized their own salvation.

When his consciousness is raised to a superior grade, there will be proper harmony between all those who live, between man and man, man and the animals and the rest of nature. There will be no difference in the field of love as all are part of divine creation even though life is at different levels.

The egotism which was the normal state of existence in the past, cause and origin of all the divisions, will have to come to an end, humanity will indeed be one family. The happy epoch will come again when the lion will eat grass with the lamb and the Earth will give fruit in abundance, so much so that a bunch of grapes would have to be carried by two men. Harmony and happiness will then reign upon Earth which is beyond all imagination.

Formal religion, as known in the past, with its divisions and its contrasts, will be a thing of the past. The infantile forms of religion in theory and in practice will be outmoded, the man of the future will have penetrated into the innermost secrets of religion which will constitute the very essence of his life.

Union will take place as well and before everything, on the level of thought, so much so that telepathy will be the usual means of communication. This will greatly enlarge agreement among human beings.

The messages of Borup tell us, however, that not everyone will be able to reach the same level at the same time. For these, another selection after a thousand years will be necessary. This will not bring death but will be on the physical plane : the second resurrection.

The true aim of evolution is to help man rise gradually from the level of an animal to that of the spirit. This will happen to those who have been found worthy to rise to the new grade. A new light will appear from these men, who will be spiritual, as spirituality will be typical of the men of tomorrow. Spirituality is above science, emotion and intelligence. Today it only belongs to the few, but it will be the dominating quality among the men of the third millennium.

The spiritual capacity will always be on the increase and the spirit will dominate the material completely.

The third millennium will have exceptional importance for the final part of Man's journey on the divine plan of evolution.

Because of the changed idea of time the thousand happy years will pass, for the new man, very quickly indeed, as several prophetically inspired communications tell us, much more quickly than in the course of the fifty thousand years of human existence beforehand. It is law that the higher that one ascends the faster is the pace. With the widening of human understanding which will become more and more vast, man will come closer to the life of the Universe and to God.

After the Thousand Years . . .

In the Superior Design that man in his present state of evolution cannot understand, everything that exists is an instrument of the Great Life.

Existence goes on in cycles always new and alternating, renewing itself at various levels, in a spiral movement growing ever greater and which will carry man ever higher.

In the vicissitudes of life every aspect will be changed. But all will live . . . for the life manifest and the life not manifest, in visible forms between the innumerable galaxies which populate the universe and in the invisible

216

forms of infinite skies.

Life is eternal ... and the Good and the Law will always continue to overcome the negative forces, the fleeing and illusory shadow of the Great Life.

IN CONCLUSION

The expectation of a harm always gives rise to fear and anxiety. That is natural. But if readers feel they have to fear the events described in this book they will not have to fear at all.

Those who know that it is fair that the dart punishes those who deserve it by design and never by chance, know too that no fear can master those who have faith in God, or those who look for the good and who are moved by a will for the good. To these peace on Earth will be brought, and not to the others; this peace which no one will be able to shatter, which no one will be able to disturb. Those who look for the good according to the teaching of Christ will have no reason to fear. All operations, however sad, are salutary as they serve to heal and then to transform in joy.

'Fear the wicked,' those who base their standards on moral or material violence, on injustice and on trickery; fear the evil ones who delude themselves that they are dominating others by the power of force or deceit, living only for the pleasures of life, and accumulate ephemeral things bitterly attacking those things which they think they will possess for all time. These people have good cause to fear and tremble, because they will be punished, because that is the best way to cure them. The Law is just, credits everyone the good to everyone always as it returns evil deeds to those who performed them. They will be punished not for revenge but for their own good, because from their personal experience they must learn to distinguish the real values of life and to choose the means for following them. The detachment from ephemeral things if not carried out consciously by one's own volition, will come as a result of the Law which is always Love.

As a result of this the believers will find themselves in the most favourable conditions: their faith will bring them into a state of happy serenity in face of whatever happens.

The contrary will happen for the unbeliever and the sceptic. 'Panic will seize my enemies,' says a message from Germany, 'and their humiliation will be without equal.'

Whatever thing will come to pass will be treated according to its own merit. Whoever wishes well need not fear whatever happens or however he feels. What matters to him persecution, cataclysms, the loss of possessions or even life itself? What matter even these terrrible events now so near when he has foreseen in times to come a higher life with a wider consciousness on the levels of the spirit?

'The evil person will have no greater enemy than himself.' (G. Bararin) and everything that strikes him will merely be his own evil actions coming back to him. We are nearing the age of the effects and no longer the causes, when everyone can act in his own sphere of freedom to modify in the conclusive moment the consequences of past errors.

Our present life is ruled by our past, just as our future is affected by how we act today. We are punished only by our own actions. They form our destiny. Everyone by his own efforts has already formed the armour to defend himself or the opening through which he will attack.

The serenity of the wise in face of the events of life is founded on the principle that, being true, they belong to all. This is the highest moral standard and very different from one founded on the fear of a God who takes His revenge, is prone to anger and partial as in the old mythology, which, besides, having passed from Judaism to the Christian world, has blotted out the idea of the true God of Love.

Certainly the Christians' ideal of love as a basis for their own actions, is of unequalled superiority, but indeed is understood and realized by only a few.

The puerile forms in which the Divinity was presented have been rightly repudiated. Nevertheless they have not been raised to a higher concept of God. If this language were used in prophecy for the people who were not very far evolved, it would be considered absolutely infantile by the men of tomorrow.

All ideas of fear of punishment and the giving of prizes belong to those who are in a state of spiritual minority and must be banned by those on a higher spiritual plane. When it is understood that the destiny of life is linked automatically to actions, it can be realized how important it is to act correctly.

Now that the world has lost all moral control either at the level of Nations or of single individuals a change is more than ever necessary. The discernment between values that are ephemeral and those that are lasting, between those who fall and those who remain, from things illusory and things real, is the best way of bringing it about. Those who have not made the choice will be under the control of forces which shake life itself whatever the future will be and will be afraid of losing the things which are being attacked.

He who believes will never lose anything because the ephemeral has no value and he will take with him everything of value. Nothing can ever touch him.

Discernment by the choice of values is the first step to start the path towards the 'high street' where no human wretchedness can ever reach.

There is one sole conclusion which is written in *The Veda*, the ancient holy books of the Orient and we offer this to the meditation of readers who wish to achieve serenity above all human vicissitudes:

'The oceans will dry up, the mountains crumble, the Pole Star fall out of the sky, the stars be ground to dust. Earth, men and gods will disappear; only the Absolute will remain!

'Oh! Man, turn towards the Absolute, which is your Destiny.'

BIBLIOGRAPHY

P. Vulliaud. *La fin du monde*. Payot, Paris, 1952.

G. Ciuffa. *La Sibille e le predizione che si vanno avver-ando*. Desclée, Rome, 1911.

H. J. Forman. *Storia della Profezia*. Sonzogno, Milan, 1939.

A. Del Fante. *La procellarie de futuro*. Bologna, 1936.

La fine dei tempi. Rivelazione urgenti de Cristo. I dischi volanti ci salveranno. Edizioni K, Rome, 1970.

Aforisimi e Presagi di Gioacchino da Fiore. Translated from the Latin by P. Baldini. G. Carabba, Lanciano, 1927.

Victor. *Profezie di tutti i tempi*. Rome, 1971.

Jean Gabriel. *San Damiano, faro di amore e di speranza*. Edizione Parvis, Bulle, Switzerland. Undated.

G. Macaluso. *Considerazioni evangeliche sulla fine del mondo*. Rome, 1964.

A. De Broglie. *Le Profezie messianche*. Con prefazione e note di A. Largent. 2 volumes. Desclée, Lefebre, Rome, 1906.

E. M. Ruir. *Nostradamus, les proches et derniers èvène-ments*. Editions Medicis, Paris, 1953.

A. Barbault (Rumelius). *Ce que sera l'avenir du monde.* Editions Fulgar, Paris, 1956.

G. Barberin. *Le profezie della Grande Piramide ovvero la fine del mondo adamitico.* Atanor, Rome, 1960.

Barberin. *L'antichristo ed il guidizio finale.* Atanor, Rome, 1960.

N. Salvaneschi. *Le Stelle, la Sfinge, la Croce. II Destina dell' Umanità.* Corbaccio dall'Oglio editore, Milan, 1952.

A. Barbault. *Les astres et l'histoire.* J. J. Pauvert, Paris, 1967.

Karmohaksis. *Le primi luce della terza era.* Rome, 1959.

F. Sanchez-Ventura y Pascual. *Le apparizioni di Garabandal.* Abete, Rome, 1967.

M. Dorato. *Gli ultimi papi e la fine del mondo nelle grandi profezie.* Rome, 1950.

V. Bruchi. *Le profezie di S. Malachia sui Papi da Celestino II (1143) a Pio XI (1939) e . . . quelli che verrano.* Libreria editrice Ticci, Siena.

Les Vrayes Centuries et prophethies de M. Michel Nostradamus etc., Rouen, 1649.

D. Piantanida. *Nostradamus predisse la fine dei tempi.* Atanor, Rome, 1969.

P. I. Rissaut. *La fine dei tempi. Profezie e predizioni di Nostradamus,* Padua, 1948.

F. Scott-Elliott. *The story of Atlantis and the lost Lemuria.* Theosophical Society, London, 1896.

Predizioni delle Dodice Sibille ecc. Ed. Giovanni Maz-
zucchelli, 1872.

J. Stearn. *The Sleeping Prophet.* Muller, London, 1971.

F. Spadafora. *Suor Elena Aiello, a Monaca Santa.* Città
Nuova edit., Rome, 1964.

R. Guénon. *La crisi del mondo moderno.* Edizioni Mediterranee, Rome, 1972.

G. Dennis. *La fine del mondo. Come? Quando? Quale
prima? E dopo?* Laterza, Bari, 1933.

A. Besant. *L'avenir imminent.* Ed. Théosophiques, Paris.
No date.

L. Christiani. *Maghi e indovini.* Ediz. Paoline, Vincenza,
1956.

R. Guardini. *La fine dell' epoca moderna.* Morcelliani,
Brescia, 1954.

D. Klitsche de la Grange Annesi. *Una mistica dell'Ot-
tocento, la Venerabile Elisabetta Canori Mora.* Rome,
1953.

T. J. Moult. *Propheties perpetuelles très curieuses et très
certains etc.* Paris, 1771.

H. J. Forman. *Les propheties à travers les Siècles.* Payot,
Paris, 1938.

R. Devigne. *Un continente scomparso: l'Atlantide,
sesta parte del mondo.* Spartaco Giovene. Milan, 1945.

*Il Vaticinatore, nuova raccolta di profezie e predizioni
etc.* Tip. Italiana di F. Martinengo. Torino, 1862.

Jeane Dixon. *My life and prophecies*. Muller, London, 1971.

M. de Sabato. *Confidenze di un veggente*. Edizioni Mediterranee, Rome, 1972.